Planning for
SUCCESS
on the JOB

Jobs of the Future ~ New Skills ~ The Right Attitude Human Relations ~ Working With Others ~ Listening Skills ~ Adjusting to the Job ~ Reliability ~ Goals Rewards ~ Chains of Command ~ Communication Networks ~ Mentors ~ Improving Your Work ~ New Employees ~ Supervisors ~ Criticism ~ Praise Anger ~ Frustration ~ Boredom ~ Discrimination Job Changes ~ Lifelong Learning ~ Burning Bridges Planning for the Future

RODGER BUSSE

Book & Cover Design: Harris Graphics
Editor/Project Coordinator: Valerie L. Harris
Assistant Editor: Joani C. Saari
Production: Valerie L. Harris, Joani C. Saari

This book was produced by Desktop Publishing techniques using Microsoft Word, and Aldus PageMaker on Macintosh computers and output to a LaserMaster 1200.

This publication is designed to provide accurate and authoritative information in regard to the subject matter covered. It is sold with the understanding that the publisher is not engaged in rendering legal, accounting or other professional service. If legal advice or other expert assistance is required, the service of a competent professional person should be sought.

Disclaimer: Information has been obtained by Career Publishing, Inc., from sources believed to be reliable. However, because of the possibility of human or mechanical error by our sources, Career Publishing, Inc., or others, Career Publishing, Inc., does not guarantee the accuracy, adequacy, or completeness of any information and is not responsible for any errors or omissions or the results obtained from the use of such information. The publisher and editors shall not be held liable in any degree for any loss or injury by any such omission, error, misprinting or ambiguity. If you have questions regarding the content of this publication, the editorial staff is available to provide information and assistance.

First Edition 1993
ISBN 0-89262-220-2
Library of Congress Catalog Card Number 93-71674

Published by

Career
PUBLISHING INCORPORATED
VOCATIONAL & APPLIED TECHNOLOGY
910 N. MAIN STREET
ORANGE, CA 92667

PRINTED AND BOUND IN THE UNITED STATES OF AMERICA

National/Canada
1 (800) 854-4014
Includes Alaska, Hawaii
and Puerto Rico

10 9 8 7 6 5 4 3 2 1

Contents

About the Author

Rodger Busse, a faculty member at Rogue Community College in Grants Pass, Oregon, has over twenty years of experience in adult education. In addition to teaching courses in Business, Supervision, and Human Relations at Work, Mr. Busse has given presentations on changes in the workplace to various state and local organizations. He has also been a speaker at the National School Boards Convention and the *Work Now and in the Future* regional workshop.

Working with the Private Industry Council, Mr. Busse has developed a variety of programs for unemployed and low-income clients, and designed training programs for medical office secretaries, legal secretaries, entry level restaurant workers and retail sales clerks. He also has worked with the Employment Division of the State of Oregon and the Private Industry Council to help retrain unemployed mill workers.

Mr. Busse's experience includes serving as Chairperson for the Ashland Schools Board of Directors, and as a founding board member of the Ashland Schools Foundation. He also has served as director of the Ashland Adult Learning Center, where he coordinated classes in basic adult education, ESL, and high school completion.

Instrumental in the development, completion, and review of over 200 training packages, Mr. Busse has helped train numerous employees of companies and organizations including 3M Corporation, Pacific Power and Light, U.S. West Communications, Southern Oregon Dental Society, United Pipe, Evergreen Savings and Loan, and the Bureau of Land Management. He currently coordinates efforts at Rogue Community College to provide customized training for businesses and organizations in southern Oregon.

A former business owner, Mr. Busse draws from his own experiences as the owner and operator of a real estate office, a restaurant, and a motorcycle dealership in offering advice to today's workers. His hands-on approach to training and education is reflected in his perspective on the changing workplace.

Acknowledgments

The development of a book involves a lot of people both directly and indirectly. My mother, Madeline Busse, taught me many lessons in life. In my early years she helped me avoid jeopardizing an opportunity for job improvement when I almost made the classic mistake of burning a bridge with my employer. As I grew up, both my mother and father shared their work experiences with me. Listening to them talk about jobs during the depression and later years helped me develop my own work ethic. Understanding *how it was* made my research into the world of work a historical review. Though she is now in her senior years, my mother is still excited about learning, and helps me organize some of my research efforts.

My wife, Patti, has been most patient with me as I spent many late nights at the computer putting my thoughts into text. She was the person I bounced ideas off of and who encouraged me to work on my book when I was distracted by other obligations and activities.

In 1984 I attended the *Work Now and in the Future* conference in Portland, Oregon. This conference about changes in the workplace featured William Daggett from New York's State Department of Education. Dr. Daggett kept me spellbound with his examples of the changing workplace—particularly in the area of technology. His early work in determining the skills needed for workers of the future sparked my interest in the whole subject of workers and the workplace.

Harold Haase is a unique person. His enthusiasm for educa-tion and learning in a real-world way is refreshing. The many hours we spent discussing the ways in which education can improve the lives of tomorrow's workers helped me maintain my enthusiasm for this project. His positive attitude and hearty laugh is infectious.

The library staff at Rogue Community College opened the doors to many new resources for me. The information used to develop the concepts and ideas in this book came from a wide variety of sources. The staff's assistance was invaluable.

Many of my colleagues at Rogue Community College helped me solidify my ideas and thoughts about this book. Their review of my outlines, suggestions, and sharing of learning materials helped me substantially with this effort.

Valerie Harris was by my side (via the phone and fax machines) most of the way. Her ideas and support are reflected throughout this effort.

Finally, Joani Saari's contributions should also be acknowledged. Her excellent proofing and editing skills are greatly appreciated.

Thanks everyone. This was a team effort.
Rodger Busse

Introduction

Planning for success on the job is not a new concept. Many workers have developed their own plans to get ahead in their place of employment. In the past, the standard for getting ahead was to work hard and do what you were told to do. Although some employees were lucky enough to work for an employer who encouraged education and self-improvement, this was not usually the case.

Today the workplace is changing in a lot of different ways. This book was designed to help you take advantage of the opportunities available to you in today's workplace and the workplace of the future. The key word is *opportunity*. Many employers are tapping the hidden abilities of their workers by encouraging personal growth through training and job advancement. That's good news! The other news is that employers now expect more of their employees.

As is the case in so many things we do in life, taking advantage of opportunity requires extra effort on our part. Today's jobs are no different. Employers expect their employees to develop and demonstrate skills that a few years ago only were required of managers. To be successful in this new environment, you will be required to learn new skills and make a commitment to continually upgrade your skills. The opportunities for success on the job are there, but you must develop a plan to take advantage of those opportunities.

Planning for Success on the Job was developed to help workers adjust to the new ways work is being done. For the worker just entering the workplace, learning the techniques and concepts presented in this book will be similar to learning any other new skill. For the veteran worker, the ideas presented may be very different from what you know about getting ahead

on the job. After you have read Chapter One, think about
what you have read in the newspapers or heard on the news.
If you have not realized this already, you will discover that jobs
and workers fill a significant portion of today's news. These
are the more obvious indications that things are changing.
If your employer has not made the changes discussed in this
book, there is a very good chance that changes are on the
horizon. Few companies will operate tomorrow the way they
do today. *NOW* is the time for you to begin developing the
skills you will need to be successful on the jobs of the future.

Note: This book will be updated periodically. If a specific
technique or method has helped you on the job, and you
would like to share it with others, please send your idea to
the author c/o Career Publishing, Inc. Our intent is to
provide the most current and useful ideas as possible to
our readers. If you can help us with that mission, we
thank you.

Chapter One:

The Changing Job Scene

Chapter Objectives

In this chapter you will:

1. Learn how the United States changed from an agricultural society to an industrial society.

2. Discover how technology and foreign competition have changed the American workplace.

3. Develop an understanding of different styles of management.

4. Learn about the skills that will be required for jobs of the future.

*There is a revolution taking place in the country
today. You won't read about it in the newspapers, nor
will you see anything about it on the evening news;
but it's taking place just the same.*

> Allen A. Schumer
> Senior Vice President, Operations
> Miller Brewing Company

The revolution that is sweeping the country is not a political
one—it is an **occupational revolution**. Today, American
workers are discovering that the jobs they have held for years
are changing rapidly. Why are jobs changing and what is
causing these changes? To answer these questions, we
must look at the history of jobs in America and at another
revolution that set the stage for today's workplace.

From Agriculture to Industry

When colonists first settled the United States, work consisted
of providing food and shelter for survival. Most jobs related
to the production and distribution of agricultural products.
Agriculture was the most important source of employment
for the colonists, and most people lived on farms. Farmers
grew the food, and **merchants** distributed it through the
marketplace to the **consumer**. Ships left the harbors of the
New World loaded with agricultural products and returned
with more people and **commercial** goods from Europe.

Ships left the new world loaded with agricultural products.

Manufacturing was limited to items crafted by skilled workers. Craftspeople made muskets, chairs, tables, dressers, silver goblets, and other items by hand, one at a time. This process required skill and patience. Because the people of the New World required little more than food, clothing, and some tools, manufacturing was not a major source of employment. Though the demand grew for products to make life easier, most of the workers were still farmers.

Workers were involved in all phases of production. Farmers planted seeds, hoed weeds, harvested crops, and delivered them to market. Raw materials were crafted into individual parts and then combined to make finished products. Children learned skills from their parents and passed them on to the next generation. Skilled workers taught **apprentices** the steps involved in the production of a quality finished product. People skilled in crafts were always in demand.

In yesterday's world of work, experienced workers taught new workers how to do all the tasks that were needed to produce a finished product. Most people worked at home or near home on the farms, and children often worked at the same jobs as their parents. It seemed that nothing would change the life of an American worker in the early days of this country—nothing except a revolution.

The revolution began with **standardized parts**—an idea first introduced in the production of muskets. Here is how it worked: Instead of one person making an entire item—piece by piece, workers made several of each part separately and then assembled the parts into a finished product. That way, if a part broke, a replacement could be obtained quickly. The process allowed American manufacturers to produce products quickly and economically with fewer skilled workers. Many factory owners used this system of production to make up for the shortage of highly skilled laborers. This system made it possible for manufacturers to meet the increasing demand for large quantities of products at lower prices.

The concept of standardized parts made it possible for an employee to focus on reproducing a single part. Employees no longer had to be trained to make every part that went into a finished product. Europeans called this system the **American system of manufacture**. This idea, which began in the United States was a totally new concept to the Europeans.

American manufacturers did not stop there; they looked for new ways to speed up the manufacturing process. Machines that could replace unskilled laborers slowly began to enter the workplace. Levers, pulleys, and gears were all devices that extended the power of workers and made them more productive. Sewing machines, spinning machines, drill presses, stamping machines, and hundreds of other machines began to change the workplace forever.

American workers shifted from being required to have a variety of skills to needing only specialized skills. Workers learned to run machines that were one part of an operation that produced a product. They labored hour after hour, repeatedly making the same part. No longer did the apprentice learn every step required to complete a musket. Instead, factory workers ran a machine that made one part of the musket, while other workers made additional parts, and still others put all the parts together. Thus, the skilled worker was replaced by the machine operator and the factory assembler.

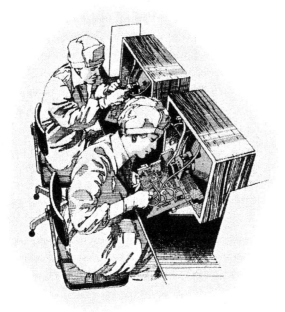

Skilled workers were replaced by machine operators and factory assemblers.

American manufacturers continued to find new ways to increase production. The **assembly line** allowed workers to put products together even faster. Workers assembled the product on a conveyor belt that moved the product past each workstation. Different workers added each part until the product was complete. At the end of the assembly line, the finished product was ready for market. Thousands of cars, chairs, guns, and tractors moved off assembly lines to meet the growing demand of American and foreign consumers.

American workers produced more than any other workers around the world. The United States became a world leader in manufacturing and technology. Quantity and low price became the driving force in American business and industry.

Machinery was introduced on the farms. Farmers began producing more crops with less effort. With fewer jobs on the farms, workers moved to the cities in search of more stable factory jobs. Agricultural jobs decreased and factory jobs increased. Life changed as the workplace changed.

The assembly line method influenced jobs outside the factory too. Store clerks learned to work in specific areas of the store known as departments, such as shoes or men's clothing. No longer did the clerk need to know all the store's stock; instead, each clerk had a specific area of concentration. The neighbor-hood grocery stores, in which the owner and employees shared all the jobs that needed to be done, were replaced by large supermarkets. In supermarkets, each worker learned only the skills that were necessary for one area or department.

*In supermarkets each worker learns only
the skills necessary for one department.*

The assembly line attitude began to penetrate all of American
society. Workers grew less and less interested in what they
were producing and concentrated only on their specific jobs.
Disinterest replaced the pride of craftsmanship. Even the
service industry concentrated on the quantity of service provided rather than the quality. Quantity and low cost replaced
quality as the formula for success in the vast majority of
American industries.

Despite the lower quality, demand for cheaper American
products grew each year. American consumers became less
concerned with quality—perhaps because it was not readily
available. Companies providing quality products and services
had become the minority.

For years, the United Stated exported more than it **imported**. Demand for American-made products increased rapidly immediately following World War II. Growth in American technology created new products to meet the endless demands of consumers. It seemed as if nothing would change the demand for American products or affect the life of American workers.

Foreign Competition Threatens American Jobs

After World War II, Germany and Japan had to rebuild their entire factory systems. Most of the factories in these countries were destroyed or badly damaged during the war. With the help of the United States, the Germans and the Japanese rebuilt their factories using the most current technology. The Japanese started using highly automated technology for manufacturing. This technology was more efficient than that used in most American factories. Furthermore, Japanese and German employees worked for lower wages than American workers. The quality of foreign products improved while prices remained competitive with similar American-made products. For the first time, American manufacturers began to experience strong foreign competition. Higher quality foreign made cameras, machinery, electronics, and other products successfully competed with lower quality American products.

The Japanese techniques and the attitude of Japanese and German workers also had a major impact on the quality of products made in these countries. This concern for quality products was the advantage foreign companies had over American businesses. Of course, many American workers did their best at their jobs, but American factory owners still required quantity over quality. Workers had little choice but to produce items as quickly as possible; therefore, few American companies achieved the same level of quality as their foreign competitors.

By the early 1970s, foreign car manufacturers were gaining a larger share of the American automobile market. Surveys of new car buyers identified quality as one of the primary reasons for buying foreign cars. American steel companies were losing millions of dollars in sales while Japanese steel production was setting new records each year. The Japanese also made high-quality television sets, stereos and other electronic products. American businesses were losing the battle with foreign competitors.

The lack of concern for quality by American workers became the subject of a number of books. These books addressed the fact that the poor quality of American cars reflected the attitudes of the workers. The assembly line was the primary cause of these attitudes. Workers did not have a sense of importance in their jobs because they played such a small role in the total production process. Factory owners made the problem worse by pushing for high levels of production with little regard for either quality or their workers. Employees complained of feeling like numbers in an organization instead of like people.

Low foreign wages allowed foreign manufacturers to **export** inexpensive foreign goods. Wages in Japan and Germany increased over the years, leading to higher prices for foreign goods; but even then, well-made foreign products proved to be too much competition for the lower quality products made by American manufacturers. Furthermore, Korea, Malaysia, Brazil, Mexico, and Taiwan joined the list of foreign competitors, forcing American businesses to rise to the challenge.

Technology Changes the American Workplace

In the 1950s, American companies began to use computers to solve problems. Many businesses used huge computers to store and direct data. These systems were very expensive and required highly trained operators.

More technological advances eventually allowed computer
designers to reduce the size of computers and lower the cost
of production. American businesses began using computers
for repetitive tasks. For example, workers who once filed
information on cards were able to use computers to file information electronically. The more computers were used, the
more new uses people found for them. Computers were able
to quickly complete many simple, repetitive tasks that used to
be done by unskilled workers. Business owners soon discovered that connected to machinery, computers could make
products with fewer mistakes at lower costs.

Several American industries, including the automobile industry, closed manufacturing plants and laid off workers during
the **recession** of 1979-83. While plants were closed, new
machines were installed, many of which were operated by
robot technology. When the plants reopened, companies did
not rehire all of the workers because some of them had been
replaced by machines. This meant the plants were able to
manufacture faster and more economically than in the past.

Technology allowed America to compete again with low foreign
wages and better quality. Now American companies could
produce quality products at competitive prices. Computer-
controlled robots and machines made parts repeatedly with
fewer mistakes.

Even expensive computer-controlled machines were not
enough to allow American companies to compete with all
foreign products. Many American businesses opened plants
overseas to take advantage of the low wages and large numbers of workers. American manufacturing had changed
forever. Companies needed a new kind of employee to work
in the high-tech factories. People with only specialized skills
could not meet the demands of the new factories. Assembly
line workers had to be retrained to use the new machines.

Computers affected all parts of the business world. Banks, insurance companies, phone companies, and department stores are only a few of the thousands of businesses that turned to computer technology to increase production and quality of service. The United States was becoming a high-tech information society competing on a world-wide level. American jobs were changing rapidly—but foreign competition remained a problem.

New Styles of Management

Many companies looked at their more successful competitors to find out how to improve their operations. Automobile manufacturers sent research groups to Japan and Germany to see why their products were more competitive than those made in the United States. They discovered that management style played a big role in product quality.

Managers in American companies continued to see their employees as part of the assembly line. American workers had little involvement in the everyday operation of their companies. In Japan, managers listened to employees' ideas and encouraged them to find new ways to make products in more efficient and less expensive ways. Companies that involved their employees in company operations reached higher levels of production than those that did not seek such input. By listening to their employees suggestions, Japanese manufacturers implemented a new management technique called a **quality circle**.

Teams of employees made up the quality circles. Each team was responsible for the quality of an entire product, not just one part. Employees learned all the steps in the manufacturing process and worked with their teams to complete products. Teams took pride in their work because they were involved in the entire process. The teams developed new and better ways to do things. Just as the colonial craftspeople took pride in the finished product, workers experienced a feeling of accomplishment—a feeling many assembly line workers had lost.

Tom Peters and Robert Waterman described such companies in their best-selling book, *In Search of Excellence* (New York: Warner Communications, 1984). These American authors described companies that allowed workers to talk directly to upper management—something unheard of in the factories of the past. These companies rewarded their employees for new ideas and encouraged them to work closely with other workers. A sense of family existed in these companies.

Another book to hit the best seller list described simple but effective management techniques. *The One Minute Manager* by Ken Blanchard and Spencer Johnson (New York: William Morrow Publishing, 1982) explained how good managers concentrated on the success of their employees as a way to succeed in business. According to the authors, good managers help their employees understand what is expected of them. They also let their employees make decisions about how to keep quality levels high while keeping up production levels. American companies that adopted these management styles experienced new levels of production. The new techniques gave workers more opportunities to use their abilities, leading to increased job satisfaction and higher quality products.

New technologies and management styles would have a lasting impact on American workers. Gone was the Industrial Revolution; a technological revolution had started. Once again, American jobs had changed, and the American worker had to change too. Just as they did in the past, today's workers must adjust to meet the new challenges of the workplace. Those workers who learn the skills needed on the job will succeed. Workers who are unwilling to change or learn new skills will not succeed in today's workplace.

Jobs of the Future

The United States is doing business in a global economy. Products and services produced in America are sold world-wide, and products from around the world are imported to the United States. Computers, **fiber optic communication** systems and **satellite communications** allow companies to do business across the ocean just as easily as they do across town. Let's look at an example of how these technological advances have changed jobs in the United States:

> Today, employees of insurance companies in New York dictate letters by satellite to China. In China, someone types the information on a computer and sends it by satellite back to the insurance companies' printer in New York. The finished letter is printed out in a matter of minutes. All this costs less than a letter typed by a secretary in the New York office where the letter was dictated. The Chinese clerk who typed the letter on the computer in China works at a much lower wage than the American secretary. This insurance company example may seem extreme, but it's only one of thousands of changes taking place because of new technology and global competition.

What does this new way of doing business mean to the American secretary? It means the American secretary must learn new skills that cannot be done by a lower paid clerk. Studies show that this is exactly what is happening.

Several major companies were asked what types of activities they required of their secretaries. The data showed that secretaries were not just typing letters and memos; they were manipulating information on computers and analyzing the results—the work managers used to do. These secretaries had learned new skills and acquired many more responsibilities. Just like the factory worker, the office worker of today no longer performs one, single task. Instead, he or she must be able to do a variety of tasks and continue to learn new skills as the responsibilities of the job change.

Technological changes are taking place all over the United States today. Let's look at another example.

For years, American Express Corporation maintained a customer service center near the company's main offices in New York City. The customer service center needed to be near the main office where all of the customer records were stored because the customer service representatives regularly spoke to customers from all over the country by telephone. They needed access to customer files to answer questions and resolve problems.

With the development of computers and telephone technology, the need to be close to the head office changed. Customer service centers could be located away from the city and still have access to customer records via computers and telephones.

So when American Express decided to build a new service center, they found they no longer needed to be close to the company's main offices. They could build in any location.

American Express hired a company to locate cities in the United States where construction costs were within their budget limits. They also wanted a place that had a surplus of workers with certain skills that American Express needed because these potential employees would require only a minimum amount of training. After looking at construction costs and qualified worker availability, American Express chose Greensboro, North Carolina for their new customer service center.

Obviously, technology and competition have changed the workplace. Jobs are changing and workers are changing with them. Developing the skills of today's worker is essential if you want to increase your chances of success on the job.

New Jobs Require New Skills

What skills will tomorrow's worker need? No one knows for sure. Our workplaces and job descriptions continue to change at a rapid rate. But that does not mean that we are totally in the dark. Clearly, whatever skills you use *now* must be improved within the next few years. So the question now becomes, "What skills am I currently using that I can build upon for my job of the future?" For a practical answer—not just a guess—let's look at the types of skills that would fit a job description of today and tomorrow:

- The employee must be self-confident.

- Workers must be alert, intelligent, well-mannered, and cooperative.

- Some technical knowledge, a positive attitude, and the willingness to learn new tasks are important.

- An employee must be an effective communicator with good verbal and writing skills. This includes proper grammar.

- He or she should dress appropriately and be well-groomed.

- Workers should have good reading and math skills, particularly in technical jobs.

- Finally, and most importantly, today's employees should develop and maintain a willingness to become involved in the company's entire operation.

Surveys conducted with hundreds of employers found these skills to be most desirable. Employers interviewing potential employees choose the person with these skills over another candidate—even if the other person has stronger technical skills. They know that the technical skills needed for future jobs will constantly change, but these basic skills will continue to be important for all jobs.

Employers also know that rapidly changing technology requires constant retraining; but training is expensive. So while most employers are willing to provide training for technological changes, they are unwilling to pay for training in the basics. Modern employers seek employees who have already developed and are using the right basic skills.

The United States Bureau of Labor Statistics predicts that soon there will be a shortage of qualified employees with basic skills. When this happens, people who have already developed the skills needed on the job today will be in even greater demand.

The secret to success is to prepare for the future by learning the proper skills as jobs change. Today's jobs are exciting, but they require employees who are prepared to handle the responsibilities and challenges of these new positions.

As managers allow employees to have more control over their jobs, employees will need to make decisions affecting, not only their jobs, but the company as a whole. Knowing how to make those decisions will be a key element in achieving success. Workers who learn all about their company provide themselves with more opportunities for new and better positions. An employee's advancement within a company will depend a great deal on how well he or she is prepared for the challenges encountered. In the chapters that follow, you will explore the many ways you can prepare for the opportunities of the future.

Study Questions

1. Most of the first jobs held by early settlers in the United States related to what?

2. In what ways was early manufacturing limited?

3. How did the concept of standardized parts change the way items were produced?

4. How did the assembly line work?

5. What caused the emphasis on the quality of American-made products to be replaced by quantity? How did this shift in emphasis affect workers' attitudes?

6. Why did foreign competition increase in the years following World War II?

7. Name some technological advances that changed the workplace.

8. How has foreign competition changed the workplace?

Chapter Two:
You Are
Your Attitude

Chapter Objectives

In this chapter you will:

1. Learn the attitudes for which employers look.

2. Develop an understanding of how a positive attitude will help you reach your full potential.

3. Find out how to develop the right attitude.

4. Learn the steps toward maintaining a positive attitude.

5. See how the right attitude can help you deal with life's challenges.

*Nothing can stop the man with the right mental
attitude from achieving his goal; nothing on earth can
help the man with the wrong mental attitude.*
                                                    Thomas Jefferson

Modern employers expect more than just basic skills from
their employees. The job skills they want in today's employee
require something special. That something special is the right
kind of **attitude**.

What is an attitude? *The American Heritage Dictionary*
(Boston: Houghton Mifflin Co., 1982) describes an attitude
as "a state of mind or feeling with regard to some matter."
What does a state of mind have to do with doing a good job?
Isn't it enough just to do what you are told to do? Frankly,
just doing what you're told is *not* enough. It is *how* you do
the job and your *attitude* toward it that count.

Employees With the Right Attitude

If you go to work each day only to do what you are told and
to receive your paycheck, you don't have the right attitude or
state of mind. Likewise, if you feel your job is unimportant
and you don't need to put much effort into your work, you
don't have the right attitude.

On the other hand, you have the *RIGHT* attitude if you look
forward to doing your job and want to do the best you can.
You also have the right attitude if your goal is to gain experience and advance within the company. People with the right
attitude want to learn as much as they can.

When employers hire new employees, they judge them by their attitudes. To today's employers, "You are your attitude." Surveys show that 80% of the job interview process depends on the impression the candidate makes during the interview. In an interview, the employer asks questions and judges the potential employee by the way those questions are answered. The candidate who answers questions with the right attitude gets the job. It's as simple as that.

Usually, the first three to six months on a job are a probationary period for an employee. The employer uses this period to decide if the employee has, or can learn, the skills that are necessary to do the job. The employer also determines if the employee has the right attitude. Employers are learning that employees with good attitudes turn out best; employees with good technical skills, but poor attitudes cause problems.

Today's employers are looking for employees who have good attitudes.

In today's competitive market, employers cannot afford problems caused by employees. Successful companies want employees who can produce as much product or service as possible with the least amount of problems: employees with the right attitude. This chapter shows you some ways you can be sure you have the right attitude.

Developing a Positive Attitude

Have you ever heard the story about two people who were asked to describe a glass of water? The first person looked at the glass and said it was half full. The second person looked at the glass and said it was half empty. It was the same glass of water, but it was viewed in two very different ways.

We call the person who saw the glass as half empty a **pessimist**. A pessimist sees the bad side of things. Another way to describe a pessimist is to say he or she is a negative person. To a pessimist, the government is all bad, the schools are a failure, and employers only care about profit—not their employees. Pessimists find fault with everything. They love to gossip about what is wrong, but seldom do they try to do anything about it. They are not fun people. They see a glass of water only as half empty, and ignore the fact that the same glass also is half full!

The person who describes the glass as half full is called an **optimist**. Optimists see the good side of things. They are positive people. Positive people tend to be the ones that get things done. They look for the good in a situation and use it to their advantage. Positive people don't dwell on their weaknesses; instead, they work on their strengths.

Productive people with disabilities often are good examples of optimists. For example, a blind man might feel sorry for himself because he cannot see the things that others see, but this would make life miserable for himself and others. So instead, he might be optimistic and concentrate on the good side of his situation; he can hear, walk, talk, and enjoy good health.

Stevie Wonder and Ray Charles are excellent examples of blind people with positive attitudes. These two famous musicians could have felt sorry for themselves because of their blindness. Instead, they took advantage of their strengths and developed their musical abilities. Today, Ray Charles and Stevie Wonder are wealthy, productive, and doing what they enjoy. If they had felt sorry for themselves and relied on others, they would not be the successful people they are today.

There are many examples of disabled people with positive attitudes. They participate in marathons in wheelchairs or with artificial limbs. Entire basketball teams are made up of players in wheelchairs. Disabled people even participate in Olympic games. Positive attitudes allow people to accomplish much more than they could with negative attitudes.

For twenty years, Napoleon Hill studied the most successful and wealthy people in the United States. Hill's goal was to find out what it was that made these people so successful. Henry Ford, John D. Rockefeller, Thomas Edison, President Woodrow Wilson, Clarence Darrow, Luther Burbank, and Alexander Graham Bell are included in those whose lives he examined.

After interviewing and studying 500 successful leaders, Hill wrote *Think And Grow Rich*—a very popular book (New York: Ballantine/Fawcett Books, 1990). In it, Hill describes a system for success developed from his twenty years of research. He pinpoints a characteristic common to 500 successful people: a *positive attitude*. Hill says these leaders were aware of the effect of a negative attitude on their abilities to succeed. Daily, they worked at maintaining a positive attitude. They knew negative attitudes influence thinking. To minimize negative influences, they constantly looked for the good in the people and things around them.

Thomas Edison exemplifies a person who maintained a positive attitude. Most people know Edison invented the phonograph, movies with sound, the electric light bulb, and hundreds of other things. But what many people don't know is that Edison had thousands of failures before he had one success. At one point, Edison's entire laboratory burned to the ground with hundreds of incomplete experiments in it. Despite this, Edison maintained a positive attitude about what he could accomplish.

Thomas Edison had a positive attitude.

If Edison had listened to the negative people around him, he probably would have given up. Instead, he told his workers to continue with their efforts because the laboratory could be rebuilt and new products could be invented.

Each of the people Napoleon Hill studied had this kind of attitude to some degree. People with positive attitudes are winners, and employers want to hire winners.

How important are positive attitudes to employers? Let's look at an example of how employees with a positive attitude affected a company's success.

Success magazine published a story titled, "The Power of Positive Thinkers," by Jill Neimark (Sept. 1987). The article described a test that Metropolitan Life Insurance Company uses to help recruit successful employees. This twenty minute test was designed specifically to identify people who have a positive, upbeat attitude. Many of the recruits who scored high on the positive attitude scale did not score high on the standard insurance exam. However, after several months on the job, the positive recruits were outselling employees hired without the use of the test for positive attitudes.

Metropolitan Life now looks for applicants with positive attitudes when they are hiring. As an employer, Metropolitan Life has found that positive employees improve the company's profits. Many popular books by successful business leaders also say that hiring employees with positive attitudes is one of the keys to success.

Why is a positive attitude so effective? Because people with positive attitudes don't give up easily. When confronted with a problem or challenge, positive employees keep trying— without relying on management to do the problem solving. This is very important to employers because they don't always have time to solve employee problems. An employer wants to be able to assign a job, and know that task will be completed quickly and accurately.   Constantly helping employees takes too much of an employer's time, and makes a company less competitive.

In addition, positive people promote good feelings within groups. If a group of employees finds the good in each other and in their work, they feel pleased and satisfied about what they are doing. They encourage each other to succeed. On the other hand, a group of employees with a negative attitude will find fault with each other or their job. An employee with a good idea may never get to try it because fellow employees find fault with it. You may have experienced this with negative people. Negative employees often are unhappy with everything and everyone around them.

Maintaining a Positive Attitude

How can you maintain a positive attitude?

Step One: Believe a positive attitude is important.
Research has shown that you will act in the way you really believe—not in what you *SAY* you believe. It is easy to say you will look for the good in people and not dwell on what's wrong, but it is much more difficult to actually do it. When fellow workers begin to complain about someone, it's easy to join in with the complainers. It's difficult not to agree, and even harder to remind the group of the employee's good traits. Similarly, when a group tells jokes about a certain employee, it's hard to walk away or resist laughing with the others. To maintain a positive attitude, you must believe that your attitude is important and act accordingly.

Step Two: Associate with positive people; avoid negative people. We are surrounded by negative thoughts and ideas. The news media looks for stories that will catch people's attention. Unfortunately, those stories usually are negative. Daily newspaper stories or television reports about murder, drugs, accidents, fraud, and child abuse tend to give us a distorted view of the world. There are many good things happening around us every day, but these usually go unreported. Thus, people get caught up in talking about what's wrong and forget to discuss what's right. Because we have so much negativism around us, it's important to associate with people who look at both sides of the story— positive people.

Positive people know there are problems in our world and are concerned about them. They also know that you don't solve problems by just looking at what's wrong. Problems are solved by identifying what is wrong and then finding ways to make it right.

Associate with positive people and let them encourage you to do your best. Let them congratulate you when you complete a task or meet a challenge. Let them share their successes with you so that you know good things are happening to others. Negativism drains energy. Positive attitudes are exciting and make you want to do more. Associate with people who get things done and who make you feel good when you are around them.

Step Three: Look for the good side in bad situations. Life will not always be pleasant. Situations will develop in which you may begin to feel sorry for yourself. You may not get a promotion you thought you were going to get, or your boss may criticize you for not working up to your full potential. It is easy to feel sorry for yourself or to blame others in these situations, but try to look for the good in what has happened.

For example, ask yourself what you can learn from not getting that promotion you wanted.   Maybe your boss didn't know you wanted it. Next time, you will develop a plan to be sure the boss knows you are interested in other job opportunities within the company. Maybe the head of the department into which you wanted to move does not know you. In the future, you will be sure to get to know people who work in other departments. That way, when a job becomes available, you will get the recommendation.

Receiving criticism from others is difficult. If your boss tells you that you are not working to your full potential, you should ask yourself why your boss feels that way. Perhaps you have become bored with your job and need to find ways to make it more exciting. You may want to discuss your job responsibilities with your supervisor. Your boss may be willing to give you an additional assignment to make your job more interesting. Trying to understand what caused a situation is much more productive than trying to blame someone or something else for that situation. Remember, you may or may not be at fault. Whatever the case, find the reasons behind any criticism; that is the surest way of avoiding more criticism in the future. Looking for the lessons that can be learned from our disappointments can help us become better people.

Employees who immediately look for someone or something to blame for their problems do not learn from their mistakes. Instead, they convince themselves that everyone else is wrong. If Thomas Edison had blamed his failed experiments on someone or something else, he never would have completed over a thousand inventions. Edison learned from his mistakes; he looked for the lesson that could be learned from a situation that appeared to be a failure. People who learn from mistakes become much wiser and better employees. Employers know this; they look for workers who know how to deal with the bad situations they encounter on the job as well as the good situations.

Your Attitude Can be Contagious

When you maintain a good attitude, others will enjoy being around you. An optimistic personality and a positive way of dealing with problems can be felt by your fellow workers and your boss. People tend to acquire the traits of others around them, so if you have a good attitude, your co-workers are likely to develop good attitudes too. Let's look at a situation that shows the effects of a positive attitude.

Alex recently was hired to work for a local department store. During the first few days on the job, he spent most of his time listening to instructions from the department manager and learning his responsibilities. When his boss asked him to stock shelves with merchandise, Alex asked questions to be sure he understood the instructions correctly. Sometimes, Alex would finish a task and be ready for a new assignment, but his boss would be busy with a customer or other employee. When this happened, Alex would look for things he could do to help other employees, such as straightening messy shelves.

One day, a customer became upset when everyone was too busy to get him some additional merchandise. Alex had finished his work and was waiting for a new assignment. Realizing that the customer was getting impatient, Alex asked if he could help him. Although Alex normally didn't work directly with customers, he knew where the additional stock was kept and found the merchandise the customer needed. When one of the other employees finished with his customer, he thanked Alex for helping.

As time passed, Alex learned more about his job and helped other employees whenever he could. More than once, he stayed a few minutes after quitting time to help the boss and other employees put merchandise away and total their cash registers. He developed a reputation for quality work and as a person who could be depended on to help whenever needed. Sometimes Alex helped other employees who were so busy they forgot to thank him.

But Alex never complained. Some employees may have even taken advantage of him by asking him to do work they may have been able to complete themselves. Again, Alex didn't complain. Instead, he used those situations to gain more experience.

On another occasion, Alex observed that his boss hated to take inventory; she was busy and taking inventory was time consuming. Realizing that inventories were a problem for his boss, Alex asked if he could learn to do them. His boss was more than happy to have someone take over the job. After only three months, Alex was promoted to a department salesperson. Today, he is a department manager.

Why was Alex so successful? Alex's boss observed the extra efforts Alex made. Other employees told the boss that they enjoyed working with Alex because he was so helpful and had such a good attitude. When a salesperson position opened, Alex was everyone's choice for the job.

If we study Alex's success story, we can see the steps that were involved in his rapid advancement. First, Alex was sincere in what he did. He didn't help other employees to impress them, he did it because he was available and they needed help.

Second, by looking for ways to help others, Alex learned more about his job and the other jobs within the department. He prepared himself for advancement.

Finally, he made his boss' job easier. Instead of waiting for the boss to tell him what to do, Alex *looked* for things to do. When other employees needed help, the boss didn't have to stop and look for someone to help the employee; Alex **volunteered**. Finally, and most importantly, Alex found something the boss didn't like to do and did it for her.

One of the things Alex did not do was take over someone
else's job or take on work he was not prepared to complete.
Sometimes employees try to do too much. This can make
other employees uneasy, and may even hurt someone.
Employees can get themselves in trouble by taking on something they shouldn't be doing. Alex was very careful to help
only when another employee needed help. He never tried to
do things just to make an impression. Instead, he helped
only when he was needed. Alex did not let his enthusiasm
for his work allow him to take on a task he couldn't handle.
The worst thing Alex could have done was try to help a
customer when he didn't know what he was doing. Alex's
success was based on doing his best and feeling good about
what he was doing.

Any employee who sincerely tries to help others, doesn't
complain about fellow employees, and strives to learn as
much as possible about the job conveys the right attitude.
As your boss and co-workers begin to notice your positive
attitude, they will begin to feel that you are fun to work
with. They will know they can trust you and depend on you.
In fact, your enthusiasm for work may help them become
more enthusiastic.

Employers today want employees who can work as team
members. They want employees who help others develop
enthusiasm. Positive employees have these characteristics
and are the people who are hired. Developing a positive
attitude is one of the keys to success.

Reaching Your Full Potential

Maintaining a positive outlook is only one aspect of a good
attitude. Believing in yourself and in what you can do affects
your attitude too. Constant attempts at self-improvement
build **self-confidence**. A number of years ago a long-distance
runner named Roger Bannister set a new world record for the

mile. He ran the mile in less than four minutes. Today,
runners make the mile run in less than four minutes on a
regular basis. What does Roger Bannister's accomplishment
have to do with attitude?

Before Bannister set his record, most people believed it was
impossible to run a mile in less than four minutes. All the
runners of the day believed that—except Roger Bannister.
He developed a plan to run each part of the race in a certain
length of time. When all the parts were put together, they
would total less than four minutes.

Roger Bannister believed he could run the mile in less than
four minutes, and he did! Within months of Bannister's
triumph, another runner broke the four-minute barrier, and
as time went on, more runners did so as well. It took Roger
Bannister to convince other runners that it could be done.
Until then, their attitudes made them believe they couldn't
run that fast. Our attitudes limit what we do.

Don't let your attitude limit you!

Often, people with negative attitudes put down people who try to do something new by telling them that the task simply cannot be done. If you are told repeatedly that you can't do something, you begin to believe it. Hundreds of experiments have shown that people limit themselves by what they believe. The limitations people place upon themselves affect the way they live their lives.

Franklin Delano Roosevelt was president of the United States during part of the Great Depression and World War II. He made decisions that improved our economy so that millions of unemployed Americans could go back to work. During the war, he met with world leaders to try to find ways to end the fighting. Roosevelt is considered one of the great leaders of modern times, yet he might have been unknown if he hadn't believed in himself.

At twenty-nine, Roosevelt was stricken with polio and left unable to walk. Many of Roosevelt's friends believed that this crippling disease would end his career. Although he worked very hard to overcome his handicap, most people believed he could never be elected President. Had Roosevelt believed this, he would not have run; moreover, he would not have succeeded. Roosevelt found ways to overcome his handicap. He didn't limit his belief in himself because of what others said. Franklin Roosevelt's attitude about himself allowed him to accomplish more than people thought he could.

Debbie Fields also believed in herself. She refused to listen to the negative attitudes of others. When Fields decided to open a store that sold only chocolate chip cookies, others said, "A store that sells only cookies? It will never work. A young woman in business? It will never work." Fields didn't listen. She didn't let other people's attitudes about women in business stop her from reaching her goal. As she thought about her business, Fields felt that people would buy her cookies if she provided the best tasting cookies and the best service.

She believed she could be successful. Debbie Fields' belief in
herself helped her become a very successful young business-
woman—in spite of what some people said.

Roger Bannister, Franklin Delano Roosevelt and Debbie Fields
all had something in common. They were able to do what
others said they couldn't. We are often told, "No, don't do
that," or, "You can't do that." Successful people do not let
such comments stop them.

Employers like employees who are willing to learn and
try new ideas. In the past, employees who limited themselves could work on assembly lines and be successful.
Today's employees are challenged to learn and grow with
the company. If they limit themselves, they are less likely
to meet their challenges. On the other hand, if they believe
in themselves, want to learn, and do their best, they will
demonstrate the characteristics of today's good employees.

By maintaining a positive attitude and refusing to limit
yourself to what others think, you gain control over your life.

Dealing With Life's Challenges

In our daily lives, we encounter a variety of challenges. Busy
schedules, deadlines, and new situations are just a few of
the daily occurrences that cause us to question our abilities
or decisions. By developing the ability to deal with these
challenges, we gain more control over our lives. Otherwise,
problems and challenges control us.

The final step in developing a good attitude is learning to deal
with problems and challenges as they arise. Generally, it is
best to try to deal with new situations as quickly and easily as
possible. Dwelling on difficulties for a long time will only
frustrate you and waste your energy, whereas rapid resolution

of your problem will bring you peace of mind. Reviewing how others deal with challenges will help you develop your own plan for dealing with difficult situations.

Angie gets along with her fellow workers most of the time. However, one day Everett, a co-worker, said something to Angie that bothered her. For several days Angie could not decide if she should say something to Everett about his comments. The more Angie thought about it, the more angry she became.

Later, Angie's boss asked her to assist Everett with some work he was doing. Without thinking, Angie said, "I doubt if he needs my help." Her surprised boss asked her why she said that.

Embarrassed, Angie apologized and told her boss that she didn't mean what she said, and quickly added that she would be glad to help Everett. Later that day, Angie told Everett that she was bothered by the comments he had made. As it turned out, Angie had misunderstood what Everett meant. She felt much better, but only after making a negative comment to her boss.

If Angie had dealt with her feelings about Everett's comments immediately, she would have realized her misunderstanding and avoided frustration and embarrassment. This was a good lesson for Angie. In the future, she will deal with situations when they arise and not let them spoil her day.

We can learn a lesson from Angie as well. If something someone says or does to you makes you unhappy, deal with it then if possible. Waiting only makes the problem bigger.

At times, however, it is better to wait before dealing with a situation. If you are very angry about something, wait until you "cool off." This is not avoiding the problem, it is simply waiting until you can deal with it in a **rational**, less emotional manner. Whether you are upset or not, the key is having a plan for dealing with difficult situations and not letting them control your life.

> Patti had worked very hard on a project for her company. After she completed the task, she took it to her boss and asked her to review it. Patti's boss studied the work and then commented that Patti hadn't followed her directions correctly, but the work basically was correct. She then went on to say that Patti didn't seem to follow directions very well.

How should Patti have dealt with the situation? She could have gotten mad at her boss and stormed out of the office. She also could have talked to the other employees about the unfairness of her boss. Instead, she thanked her boss for the information, waited a few minutes to calm down, then returned to her boss' office.

Patti explained that she wasn't sure what she had done incorrectly and asked her boss to help her avoid this problem in the future. Patti made it clear that she wasn't necessarily disagreeing with her boss, but that she wanted to understand the problem better. As Patti's boss tried to explain what she felt Patti should have done, the boss realized she hadn't really spent enough time explaining what she wanted. Furthermore, the boss admitted she had been very busy and appreciated the fact that Patti finished the project without needing a lot of additional help. Patti's boss promised to spend a little extra time explaining future assignments.

Your attitude is a combination of many factors. Together, these factors make up the *you* that people know. If you join a group that puts down others, then that is the *you* that people know. If you are always afraid to try new challenges because you are afraid of failing or making a mistake, then that is the *you* people know. If you worry and fret about things, using up valuable energy, then that is the *you* people know.

On the other hand, if you feel good about yourself, remain optimistic, and deal with problems when they happen, then that is the kind of person your boss and fellow employees will know. Which one do you want to be? The choice is yours. Remember, *you* are your attitude.

You ARE your attitude!

Study Questions

1. What type of person has the attitude for which employers look?

2. List three steps that will help you maintain a positive attitude.

3. How can having a negative attitude affect your job?

4. Often, we face challenges or difficult situations. How can we keep these from controlling us?

Chapter Three:

Human Relations at Work

Chapter Objectives

In this chapter you will:

1. Discover the importance of working well with others.

2. Learn how to develop good listening skills.

3. Learn how to work well with your boss.

4. Find out how to be someone with whom other people enjoy working.

*Each team manages everything from its own budget
and inventory control to hiring, without direct over-
sight from top management.*
> David Woodruff,
> in a description of Saturn
> Automobile Corporation work teams

Productive Employees
Make a Company Successful

An advertisement on television portrays a gray haired man
claiming that he liked the electric razor he is holding so
much, he bought the company! The advertisement is for
the Remington Razor, and the speaker is Victor Kiam,
president of Remington Products, Incorporated. The story
of Mr. Kiam's success with Remington is about **teamwork**.

The Remington Company produced electric razors for many
years. By the end of the 1970s, Remington was the only
electric razor made in the United States. All the other American companies had gone out of business and Remington was
in trouble, losing millions of dollars a year. It appeared that
Remington would go out of business too.

Victor Kiam invested all his money when he purchased the
Remington Company. He believed he could turn the company
around and make it **profitable**. In less than two years, Victor
Kiam turned Remington Products, Inc. into a highly profitable
business. How did he accomplish this major success? Kiam
saved the Remington company by improving its **efficiency**.
One of the most important steps he took was to allow his
employees to work toward their full **potential**.

In his book, *Going For It* (New York: William Morrow Publishing, 1986), Kiam describes how important his employees were to his success. He explains, "And, of course, there were the people, the Remington employees. The **turnaround** wasn't my triumph; it was our triumph. Those hard-working loyalists teamed up with this **entrepreneur** to prove all the experts wrong." Victor Kiam understood the importance of teamwork. So do many other employers today.

In the media, we hear about the efforts many companies are making to involve their employees in more of the company's operation. **Quality circles** and **participatory management** are terms that frequently to describe this employee involvement. Today's worker is becoming increasingly important to a company's success.

Employee teams can help set new production records.

Competition in the United States and from other parts of the world is forcing companies to become more efficient. As businesses **automate** their operations, they depend more on employees to make decisions on the job. Teamwork allows American companies to stay competitive.

Working in Teams

Today's jobs require employees to work successfully with each other. Employers are discovering that employees working in teams are more efficient than employees working alone. In the past, assembly line workers did one task all day long. Today's employees do a variety of tasks, many of which call for **cooperation** between co-workers.

Sometimes it is easier to work by yourself than it is with someone else. When you work alone, you can work at your own speed and do things the way you want. Working with someone else requires special skills. Each person has his or her way of doing things. If you are going to work successfully with others, you need to realize the importance of finding out how your co-workers think something should be done. Your way may be better, but you may have to **compromise** when you work with someone else.

Compromising means that each person makes adjustments to the way they want to accomplish a task. It does not always mean doing something the way someone else wants to do it. The task is completed by working together and using ideas from each person. Compromising saves time, and often gets the job done more effectively.

Learning to work with fellow employees offers an extra benefit. You learn faster and easier and often find better ways to accomplish a task. People usually attempt to complete a task by applying knowledge they have gained from past experiences. By working with other employees, you can use their experience as well as your own to complete a task. This way, you gain new job experience from a co-worker, and your co-worker has received new information from you.

Learning is a wonderful process. By learning, employees become more valuable to their employers. Employers are looking for employees who work well with others because it speeds up the learning process, and ultimately leads to greater productivity. Two or more people working together usually are more effective than one person working alone. Working in teams is proving to be an effective way to solve problems and get things done efficiently.

Today's employers are looking for
employees who can work well with others.

The Importance of Good Listening Skills

Some of the most important skills to learn when you work with others are those of a good listener. Most people are not good listeners; and yet these skills are needed every day. Listening skills are necessary whenever you receive instructions from another person—especially if you will be required to repeat or explain them to someone else. Bosses don't have much patience with employees who don't listen. Failure to listen carefully leads to mistakes.

Good listeners generally have effective discussions with other employees. If you are working on a group project, your group may need to determine the best way to carry out the task. If you listen to the people in your group, you will probably learn something new; or maybe you will hear something that will give you new ideas. Even if you are the most experienced member of the group, you will benefit by listening to others.

Improving Your Listening Skills

Becoming a good listener takes practice. Many studies have been done on the development of listening skills. These studies identify the following techniques as keys to good listening:

1. **Look at the person who is talking to you.** If your eyes wander away from the speaker, your mind will follow. When you are distracted, you miss important information. Therefore, you must *concentrate* on everything that is said. Furthermore, when you look away, you convey a **subtle** message to the speaker that what he or she is saying does not interest you. Do you want to give this message to your boss or fellow employee?

2. **Ask questions when you don't understand.** If you don't understand what the person is saying, ask a question that will help you understand the explanation. Wait for the speaker to pause; then ask the speaker to repeat what was said or to explain it in a slightly different manner. Try not to interrupt, but don't wait too long to ask your question. A long wait will make it hard for you to understand the entire explanation.

   Some employees are afraid to ask questions when they are given directions. They mistakenly believe it will make them look stupid to their boss or another employee. The truth is, asking questions shows that you are paying attention and want to get the correct information.

   Asking questions will help you understand what the person is saying and it tells the speaker that you are interested in what he or she is saying. In addition, by asking questions you are creating better working relationships with fellow employees and your boss.

3. **Avoid interrupting the speaker.** Since almost everyone likes to talk, this is a problem for many people. Unfortunately, you can't talk and listen at the same time. When you listen to someone speak, you may think of things you would like to say in response. You may even think that what you have to say is more important than what the speaker is saying. Resist this feeling. Wait until the speaker is finished, then address your point. If you do not, you may miss out on valuable information and neither you nor the speaker will receive an entire message.

   For example: Ryan is telling John how to repair a broken compact disc player. As John listens, he thinks about equipment he has fixed in the past. Soon, John is telling about all the things he has fixed. Ryan is trying to help John, but John is showing that he isn't interested. He was too busy talking about himself. Consequently, John does not learn how to fix the CD player, and Ryan will think twice before explaining anything to John again. Remember, you are the listener—listen!

4. **Don't think about your answer while listening to the speaker.** As you listen to someone, you may start planning your response to what is being said. This is especially apt to happen if someone expresses a viewpoint with which you do not agree. However, if you are not careful, you might find that you are no longer listening. Instead, you are waiting for the speaker to pause so you can disagree.

   Thinking about your answer instead of listening can create embarrassing situations. You might find that because you were not listening carefully, your response contains some information that is the same as what was just said to you. When this happens, you not only miss what the other person has to say, but you imply that what was being said isn't important to you. This does nothing to build a good working relationship with fellow workers!

5. **Watch out for *trigger* words.** Most of us are sensitive to certain words. These words can trigger a reaction that distracts us from the speaker. A trigger word can be as common as the word *vacation*. That word may start you thinking about your vacation and stop you from listening to the speaker. There is nothing wrong with reacting to a certain word; it is human nature. The problem arises when you dwell on the word or on its significance and stop listening to the speaker.

Words that are likely to cause a reaction in a listener may refer to race, gender, political parties, social levels, etc. The more you think about trigger words, the less you hear the speaker. Your overreaction affects your listening skills, and you do not hear what is being said. It may not be the speaker's intention to distract you with these words. In fact, the speaker may not even be aware that he or she has said something that disturbs you. Be aware of trigger words and don't let them distract you from being a good listener.

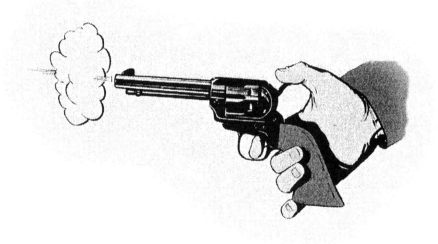

Watch out for trigger words!

6.   **Evaluate the message instead of the speaker.** We
     hear a lot about short people, tall people, fat people,
     skinny people, people who dress well, and people who
     look poor. These physical descriptions lead to labels we
     place on others. Because of these labels, we sometimes
     judge what people are saying by the way they look.

     Have you ever listened to someone explain something
     complex and said to yourself, "That person doesn't look
     smart enough to know that?" If your boss always came
     to work looking messy, would you judge the importance
     of his or her instructions by the way your boss looked?

     Here is an example of how evaluating a person by his
     appearance can lead to an undesired result.

> A car salesman once thought he knew his customer in
> spite of what the customer was saying. The customer
> entered the automobile dealership dressed in coveralls
> and worn-out boots, saying he wanted to look at a new
> Cadillac and would pay cash if he liked the car. He went
> on to say his farming business had been good that year
> and he deserved a new car. He had stopped by to look
> at cars on his way to the farm supply store.
>
> The salesman didn't listen to what the man was saying;
> instead, he decided this person was dressed too poorly to
> buy a Cadillac. He probably drove an old pickup truck.
> Have you guessed what happened? The salesman didn't
> spend any time with the poorly dressed customer. As it
> turned out, the customer was one of the wealthiest
> farmers in the county and *did* pay cash for a new car—
> elsewhere!

Evaluate the message—not the speaker.

7. **Make an uninteresting subject interesting by asking yourself questions.** There will be times when you will have to listen to information that seems uninteresting. For example, your boss may feel that it's important to explain a company policy you already understand; or a co-worker may need to demonstrate a task that does not interest you. How can you make these discussions and others interesting?

Ask yourself questions about the subject matter being discussed. You might ask yourself, "Why does my boss think this policy is so important? Has there been a problem in this area?" As you listen to the speaker, listen for the answer to your questions. You will pay closer attention to a speaker if you are listening for answers. It makes the information more interesting. Try this technique next time you think you are losing interest in a speaker. It works!

Make uninteresting information interesting
by asking yourself questions.

8. **Don't let emotional words distract you.** An emotional word or phrase is one that affects someone's feelings rather than appealing to their sense of logic. Emotional words can distract you in the same way as trigger words. They differ from trigger words in that they affect you on a more personal level. Here is an example of a listener who became distracted by emotional words:

> Ryan was upset with Linda because she had not completed the report he needed. He said, "You're not finished yet? Please don't let me down—I really need that report." He then went on to explain that he could wait one more day for the report.
>
> Linda did not hear Ryan's very important final words. She was thinking about his words "not finished" and "let me down." She heard those words over and over, but not the other words Ryan was saying. Instead, Linda was thinking, "Doesn't he know how busy I am?" Finally Linda replied, "If that is the way you feel, I'll work late tonight and finish the report by tomorrow. It's too bad you couldn't give me a little more time so I wouldn't have to work tonight!"
>
> Ryan looked at Linda and didn't say anything for a long moment. Finally, he said, "Didn't you hear me? I just said you could have another day to complete the report."
>
> Linda was very embarrassed. She had not listened to Ryan carefully.

Linda let emotional words distract her. Don't let emotional words distract you. Be a good listener.

Don't let emotional words make you a poor listener.

9. **Control a wandering mind.** Everyone has this prob-
    lem at some time or another. It is easy to be distracted
    and start thinking about something else. You may
    think about what a beautiful day it is, how warm or
    cool you feel, or hundreds of other things. Why do we
    let our minds wander?

    The human brain can process a great deal of informa-
    tion at once. For instance, it is possible for you to read
    this sentence, sense the temperature in the room, hear
    a person near you breathing, and notice how hard and
    uncomfortable your chair is—all at the same time.
    How does this capacity affect the way we listen?

Americans speak in conversations at the rate of about 125 words per minute. However, a person can listen at a rate of approximately 400 to 500 words per minute! So what do you do when someone is talking to you at 125 words per minute? Your brain needs more information to process; so your mind leaves the conversation, and thinks about how warm it is in the room and how you wish someone would open a window. After a moment or two of this side thought, your full attention returns to the speaker. If you were distracted only for a moment, you can pick up the speaker's words and still understand everything that is being said. Unfortunately, however, we don't always return to listening to the speaker quickly enough. If you have missed too much, the speaker's words won't make sense. A wandering mind can make you a poor listener. How can you keep your mind from wandering?

Concentrating on the speaker will help you overcome the tendency to let your mind wander. Thinking about the ideas presented by the speaker will keep your brain busy. It also helps to make quick mental summaries of what the speaker is saying at intervals. Put ideas and thoughts together. Remember, the speaker is using words to create ideas and thoughts for you. As a good listener, you need to put these thoughts and ideas together so they make sense to you. *Concentrate* and become an outstanding listener.

10. **Be aware of good listening techniques.** Being a good listener requires extra effort. The techniques listed here can help you improve your listening skills. Take a few minutes and think about your listening habits. Do you look at the person who is speaking to you? Do you avoid distractions? As you review your habits, identify those techniques that will help you improve your ability to listen. Select one or two to practice as

you listen to others. As your listening skills improve, move on to another technique. Over time, you will improve all your listening skills. The secret to learning any new skill is to realize that it is easy to go back to your old way of doing things. Continually remind yourself of the importance of being a good listener.

People like good listeners and want to work with them. If you listen carefully to what people are saying, you will know more about them and what they do. The more you listen, the more you can learn from others. With knowledge about other workers and the company operation, you become an important and valuable part of the company.

Learning How to Work With Your Boss

In addition to working well with co-workers, good employees must know how to work with their boss. Some bosses have good people skills and others do not. Today many managers are concerned about having a positive working relationship with their employees. On the other hand, some managers still believe that workers should carry out directions with no questions asked. Regardless of the type of boss you have, communication with him or her is very important.

Learning about your boss will make it easier to work with her or him. Many employees never really understand their bosses. Often there is more than one way to complete a task. However, a boss may prefer the job to be done a particular way. A good employee should try to do it that way. Doing it differently from what the boss wants does not help when pay raises are being considered or promotion opportunities arise. Let's look at the management styles that are common in the workplace and the best way to work with each.

Today many managers believe in *participatory management.* This style of management allows the worker to **participate** in management decisions. Participatory managers will ask employees to work with other employees to complete a task. They expect their employees to make decisions regarding work responsibilities. The more experienced the employee, the more decisions he or she will be allowed to make. Employees who work for a participatory manager usually are allowed to be very creative and suggest new ways to do things. This style of management provides employees with the greatest opportunity for personal growth on the job.

Working for a boss who allows employees to make decisions has its pitfalls. Bosses sometimes lose patience with employees who cannot make decisions. If you ever feel overwhelmed by the decisions you are asked to make, you should talk to your supervisors about your concern. Feeling uncomfortable about an assignment or task may mean that you don't fully understand the assignment. Or, it may mean that you don't have enough experience to make the right decisions. A good manager only will allow an employee to make decisions that are within that employee's ability and experience.

Participatory managers look for employees who can lead others. This ability is called *leadership.* Employees who possess leadership skills are always in demand because they can be depended on to get a job done without a lot of help from the boss. Leadership involves taking the **initiative** to get a task done. It may include other employees. An employee with good leadership skills knows how to tackle an assignment and involve others in getting the job done.

Being allowed to take a leadership role on the job is very exciting. It also involves a lot of responsibility. If a boss allows a worker to take the lead on a job, the boss expects the job to be done properly. If you are unsure of your ability to accept all the responsibility, discuss it with your boss. He or she should give you the support you need to complete the task successfully. Asking for help is not a sign of weakness; it is a sign that you want to do the job right.

An **authoritarian** is someone who demands full authority in all situations. An **authoritarian style of management** is the opposite of a participatory style of management. It is typically used in very disciplined environments. Army generals are authoritarians. They give directions and expect soldiers to follow those directions exactly. In a crisis, a police sergeant gives junior officers directions and expects them to be carried out quickly and without question. These are unique situations, but some managers still believe this is a good approach to managing workers. This style of management is rapidly being replaced by methods that allow more input from employees.

Often, a manager will vary his or her style of management, depending on the situation. If the employee is new and inexperienced, the manager may give very specific directions. On the other hand, experienced employees may be given very little direction and allowed to do the work on their own. There is no single right way to manage people.

The key to working well with your boss is to learn the style of management he or she uses. If you are new on the job, pay particular attention to your boss' methods of working with other employees. Is everyone treated the same? How much freedom is given to experienced employees? As you begin to learn your boss' style, think about what you can do to fit in with that style of leadership.

If your boss is the type who tends to give directions and does not let employees make suggestions, look for different ways of approaching new ideas. Instead of voicing your ideas, try asking a question that will help your boss get the idea.

Rosemary had a good idea that would save the telemarketing company time in recording telephone messages; but her boss, Kathy, was not open to employees making suggestions. How could Rosemary get her message across without upsetting her boss? She could ask a question.

So Rosemary asked, "Would it be any faster if we typed messages on the computer and made several copies for the office staff?" Her boss realized that Rosemary's idea was a good one. Kathy told Rosemary the method probably would work and that Rosemary could try it if she wished. What did Rosemary accomplish? First, she was able to change the system to everyone's advantage. Second, her boss liked the idea but was still able to feel in control. Third, as time passes, Kathy will have more confidence in Rosemary because her questions lead to improvements in the office. She may even begin asking Rosemary for ideas to improve office operation. Bosses can learn from employees too!

If Rosemary had presented the idea as her own, her boss probably would have rejected the idea. In addition, her boss might have resented Rosemary even suggesting a change. By understanding Kathy's management style, Rosemary was able to make a change and stay on the good side of her boss.

Not all situations will work out this well; your boss may not agree with an idea. If this happens, it is best to accept the situation and wait for another opportunity to present the idea.

Mack works for a boss who doesn't want to be bothered with problems. His method of working with his boss is to find out what needs to be done and then do it. He doesn't bother his boss unless he is not sure how his boss may want the job finished. Mack's boss knows that Mack doesn't ask questions unless they are important. If Mack didn't know his boss' management style, he might ask too many unnecessary questions—and try his boss' patience.

Successful employees soon learn the best ways to work with their bosses. They know how to strengthen employer/employee relations. Good employees also realize that bosses are human. Like everyone, bosses have good days and bad days. Being sensitive to your boss' feelings will help you **cultivate** good relations. If your supervisor seems down, be positive. If he or she mentions that profits are down and the company needs to cut costs, don't pick that day to ask for a raise. If the boss seems upset about something, don't bring up a problem—unless it cannot wait for another time. Bosses have a variety of problems and situations to deal with every day. Recognize these situations and try not to make them *more* difficult for your boss to handle.

Knowing your employer's management style will make you a valuable employee. Your boss will feel comfortable working with you and will recommend you for more responsibility. Working well with your boss is like working well with other employees; it makes your job more exciting and challenging. You can work against others or you can work with them. It is both easier and more rewarding to work together.

Learn your boss' management style.

Working Well With Others

Working with others can be a challenge at times because everyone has their good days and bad days. But making the extra effort to be someone with whom everyone likes to work will pay off over time. The ability to adjust to others and work with a variety of people is an important skill for an employee to possess.

Being **sensitive** to the feelings of others is a key element in good human relations. If your boss or fellow worker arrives at work upset because of a flat tire, be sensitive to those feelings. It is not good to discuss something that may have gone wrong the preceding day at times like this. If possible, wait until the person who is upset has recovered from the experience.

Avoid bringing personal problems with you to work. Personal problems will interfere with your job performance and may even distract others. Sometimes other employees will come to work upset by problems at home. Try not to get involved when another employee is upset. Just deal with him or her the best you can. If the problem continues, it will be the supervisor's responsibility to help the employee realize that personal problems are affecting his or her job performance.

When you work for a company that has several employees, you will encounter a variety of personalities. Each person you work with will have unique personal characteristics. Learning how to deal with these differences is part of being a good employee. It's not the boss' responsibility to make others get along with you. It is *your* responsibility to find the best way to work with your boss and other employees.

Dealing with difficult people can be challenging. Instead of getting angry or frustrated with someone, use the situation to improve yourself. Consider it a challenge and figure out a way to work together. Over time, you will be happier at work and you will improve your **reputation** as a good employee.

Have you ever looked at a clown and not smiled? Most clowns have big smiles painted on their faces. It's hard not to smile when you see someone else smile. Smiling makes you feel good and it makes those who work with you feel good too. People enjoy being around you when you look happy. Of course, you can't be happy all the time; however, if you feel good about yourself, your job, and the people you work with, that smile will be there most of the time. If you dislike your work, or let other unhappy people influence your attitude, you are more likely to wear a frown.

Part of being and looking happy is having a good sense of humor. A person with a good sense of humor is generally open and friendly with others. It isn't necessary to know a lot of great jokes; a light-hearted attitude with co-workers is a sign of a good sense of humor. If you hear a funny story, share it with the people around you. At national speech contests, the winning speech is almost always humorous. Keep in mind, however, that a story you think is funny might not be funny at all to someone else. Avoid telling stories or jokes that might offend someone. It is also important to make sure that your sense of fun does not interfere with work.

People will enjoy being around you if you have a sense of humor. Try to find the humor in difficult situations, and don't be afraid to laugh at yourself. Political candidates with a good sense of humor have a much better chance of being elected. Be optimistic and don't take disappointments too seriously. Enjoy life!

Smile—its contagious!

The ability to work with others is an important part of being a productive employee. Remember—to be a valuable team member, you must learn to compromise, cooperate, and listen. By applying these techniques, and maintaining good humor, you can reinforce your reputation as a good employee and become a real asset to your employer.

Study Questions

1.   Who does Victor Kiam credit with the turnaround of Remington Products, Inc.?

2.   Describe some benefits of learning to work with others.

3.   List the keys to good listening.

4.   What is *participatory management*?

5.   What is an *authoritarian style of management*?

6.   Why is it important to learn your boss' style of management?

7.   Sensitivity and a sense of humor are important personality traits. Describe a situation in which either of these can help create a more efficient workplace.

Chapter Four:

Being a Good Employee

Chapter Objectives

In this chapter you will:

1. Discover the traits employers look for in an employee.

2. Find out how to develop a reputation for reliability.

3. Learn how to praise yourself and others.

The answers to three questions will determine your success or failure. 1. Can people trust me to do my best? 2. Am I committed to the task at hand? 3. Do I care about other people and show it? If the answers to these questions are "yes," there is no way you can fail.

Lou Holtz
Notre Dame football coach

Employers are Looking for Good Employees

Have you ever thought about what it would be like to own a bank? People would come to your bank and deposit their money into savings and checking accounts. Your bank would then loan that money to other customers. These customers would use the money to buy houses, cars, boats, pay for vacations, college tuition, and other needs they have.

As the owner, you would hire people to help run the bank. Tellers would help the customers when they come in to make deposits and withdrawals. Loan officers would review customers' loan applications and approve loans to meet the customers' needs. Clerks would work in the accounting department to keep track of the bank's money and pay the bank's bills. Employees in the personnel department would hire new employees and fire others who are not good workers. Other workers would be in charge of payroll, and still others would be responsible for filling out state and federal forms needed to run the bank. You would also need to hire managers for the different departments and security officers. Like any business owner, a bank owner's goal is to make a profit. To make that profit, all the bank's operations must be carried out efficiently.

Let's look at a simplified version of the way a successful bank operates.

Employees arrive before the bank opens to prepare everything for the customers who arrive at 9 a.m. Tellers put cash in their cash drawers, turn on their computers, check in with the main computer, and gather the materials they will need to process customers' deposits in their checking and savings accounts. Other employees may work in New Accounts. These workers must be prepared to make it easy for customers to open new checking and savings accounts.

Before the bank opens each morning, loan officers meet and look at the current interest rates for loans. They also may have to review other applications for approval. Paperwork must be filled out and ready for the customers' signatures when they arrive, and money must be ready for the customers whose loan applications have already been approved.

Throughout the day, clerks and bookkeepers work on payroll records to prepare paychecks for employees. Meanwhile, an accountant or bookkeeper may review the bank's books to prepare reports for state or federal **auditors**. Another book-keeper may write checks to pay the bank's bills.

As a banker, people would trust you with their money and depend on you to lend them money when they need it. You would pay your customers **interest** for putting their money in your bank, and you would charge a little more interest to lend customers money for their needs.

If each operation was completed properly, you would make a profit and your bank would be successful. You would plan all the bank's operations to make sure that you always made more money than you spent.

For example, if it costs five million dollars a year to run your bank and pay all the bills, you will have to be sure your bank's operation brings in more than five million dollars. This way, the bank makes a profit.

Any business that has employees has a set of operations that make the business work properly. The employees are responsible for carrying out the business operations on a daily basis. If an employee fails to complete an operation, the business suffers. Could one employee make your bank lose money? How about two or three? How many inefficient employees can your bank withstand before it begins to lose money? Let's see how employees can affect the success of any business.

One of the most important employees in a bank is the teller. Bank customers meet with the teller whenever they come in to access an account. If one of your tellers fails to show up for work, it means all the other tellers must work extra hard to take care of the missing teller's customers. In addition, the customers must wait in longer lines because one teller is missing. What if two tellers don't show up for work? You now have even longer lines and tellers who are under more pressure to meet all the customers' needs. Tellers who have to work harder get tired faster; they lose patience with customers and are not as friendly as they should be.

If your bank has tellers who are absent on a regular basis, your customers will get upset with the extra wait in line and the unfriendly tellers. They may even go to another bank! What if a teller is late? The same problem exists—one teller window is not ready when the customers arrive. The other tellers must deal with an additional workload until the late teller arrives.

A bank is only as good as its employees.

Other departments in the bank depend on employees for their day to day operation as well. If the bookkeeper who prepares the report for auditors doesn't show up for work, someone else has to do the job. If the payroll clerk doesn't get the pay checks out by payday, the other employees will be upset and may be unfriendly with the customers.

A loan officer may be having problems in his or her personal life and call in sick every Monday. This means the other loan officers have to work extra hours to process the missing officer's loans and meet with extra customers. Customers will have to wait longer to see a loan officer, leading some of them to start doing business with another bank.

When employees don't carry out their job responsibilities, they create problems for everyone else, and ultimately, the business suffers. If too many customers are lost, business drops off and less money is made than it takes to run the business; therefore, no profit is made. No matter how good the procedures and operations are, poor employees will affect the success of any business.

Even one employee can have a negative influence on a business. It takes a while for a new business to make enough money to pay the bills and make a profit. If one employee is unfriendly or doesn't do his or her job properly, the customers you are trying to acquire may not come back. Without new customers, the business will fail or show a limited profit. If the business fails, all the employees will lose their jobs, not just the employee who didn't do his or her work.

If you had a business that was suffering due to a problem employee, what would you do? You probably would replace that employee. Most business owners are aware of the problems that poor employees can create, so they try to hire good employees from the beginning. They can't afford to let employees' problems affect their businesses. As Harold Haase, president of Career Publishing, Inc., says, "You gotta have a good attitude to work here!"

Today, good employees are critical to the success of American businesses. Competition from other businesses locally, nationally and globally has forced many companies to pay more attention to the quality of the employees they hire. Now, more than at any other time in our history, companies are relying on quality employees to help them succeed in business.

In many parts of the country, businesses are experiencing a shortage of *good* workers. In New York City, Chemical Bank must interview forty applicants to find one that can be successfully trained as a teller. Estimates indicate that by the year 2000, the United States will have a severe shortage of **qualified workers**.

The decline in the supply of qualified workers is, in part, due to rapid technological change. Technology is changing the workplace faster than people can be trained to fill the new jobs. As population growth levels off, this shortage will become even more acute. How can you take advantage of this situation? What skills can you develop to become a good qualified worker?

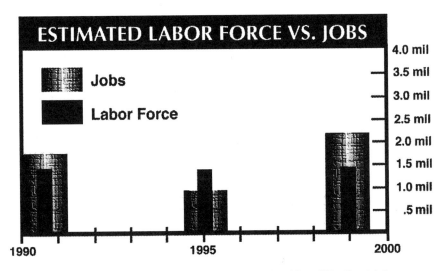

SOURCE: United States Bureau of Labor Statistics; Adapted from "The Great Jobs Mismatch" by Robert J. Shapiro & Maureen Walsh. *(U.S. News & World Report*, Sept. 7, 1987.)

The numbers of qualified workers will
decline over the next few years.

Adjusting to a New Job

Starting a new job can be both fun and frustrating. You will be required to learn new skills and to learn about the company in a short period of time. The fun part is learning new things. The frustrating part can be trying to learn a lot of information quickly. What are some ways you can learn quickly without becoming frustrated?

Using your listening and questioning skills is the secret to learning quickly. As someone explains something to you, listen carefully. If you are not sure of something they said, ask questions or **paraphrase**. If the explanation is simple, you may only need to ask a question now and then. However, if the explanation is more complex, paraphrasing may be helpful. Paraphrasing is a technique that can be used when you want to be sure you understand what has been said.

To paraphrase someone, repeat what the speaker said in your own words. It works like this. Randa is explaining to Jose how to prepare a report for the advertising department, but Jose is not sure he understands the last part of the explanation. To clarify his understanding, Jose says, "Let me see if I understand the last part of your explanation: I need to prepare three copies of my report for the sales department; one copy goes to the supervisor of the department, one to the department secretary, and one copy remains in our department file." Randa might agree with Jose's understanding, or she might make a slight correction.

Randa might correct Jose's paraphrase by saying, "The third copy goes in the sales department file, *not* our department's file." Now Jose clearly understands the steps involved in preparing the reports. If Jose had asked the simple question, "I need to make three copies of the report—is that right?" Randa would have agreed with Jose's question. Unfortunately, Jose wouldn't understand all the directions and would have put the report in the wrong file.

We all make some mistakes when we are learning new things. By asking questions and paraphrasing, we can limit the number of mistakes we make.

Learning information ahead of time will speed up the process of adjusting to the job. If there are opportunities to learn more about the company, take advantage of them. This way, you don't have to wait for others to give you information you need—you'll find out for yourself.

If you are having lunch with other employees, ask them about themselves and their jobs. People like to feel that others are interested in them and in what they do. Unless they are unsociable, they will be anxious to tell you about themselves. Ask questions of different people. Don't corner one person to answer all your questions. Make all your contacts with others an opportunity to learn information ahead of time.

Learn about your job by listening
to others discuss their work.

As time goes on, you will have opportunities to learn more about your job by being curious. The more you learn on your own, the less time others will need to spend teaching you about your job. Furthermore, by asking questions about your job, you show an interest in the company and fellow employees. Be **sincere** in your efforts to learn more about others and the company. If you are asking questions to impress others, it may backfire on you—they may think you are just showing off. Your questions must be asked because you honestly want to gain more information. The more you learn, the faster you become a valuable employee.

Another way to learn quickly is to be a good listener. You don't always have to ask questions to be a quick learner. Often, listening to the conversations of others may provide you with information that will help you on the job. Be careful though! Don't be an **eavesdropper**. Do not listen in on private conversations or business concerns that are not intended for your ears.

By listening to others discuss their work and the company, you can quickly gain a better understanding of your job. While eating lunch, you may hear other employees discussing a problem they encountered on the job and their solution to the problem. The time may come when you encounter a similar problem and you will already have a solution!

Frequently, a new employee is so busy talking about themselves, they miss opportunities to gain valuable information by listening to others discuss their work. Don't feel that you have to impress your fellow workers in order to be accepted by them. Showing an interest in those you work with is much more effective.

It is important for a new employee to be accepted by others as quickly as possible. One way to speed this process is to learn the names of other employees. Learning names is often just a matter of being a good listener. By listening to conversations between others, you can associate names with faces. If you can later address that person by name, you have taken a major step toward being accepted by those you work with on a daily basis.

Developing a Reputation for Reliability

In our bank example, we saw how much everyone in an organization depends on other employees to complete their jobs. Your employer, as well as other employees will want you as part of the organization if they can depend on you to get the job done. When a boss gives you an assignment, he or she needs to know you will be there on time to complete the assignment correctly. If you don't come to work on time or are absent a great deal, someone else will have to do your work. No one wants to work with an unreliable person. How can you develop a reputation for **reliability**?

The first step toward being reliable is to understand how important you are to the organization. By learning the importance of your job, you will better understand why you need to be at work on time and on a regular basis. Many employees have the mistaken belief that their job is not important and that it won't make much difference if they do not show up for work. These employees do not understand how their job relates to the rest of the company.

Whenever you are not at work, someone else has to carry out your duties for you. If you are ill and can't go to work, or if you are going to be late due to a situation beyond your control, call your employer and explain the situation. This will give him or her a chance to find someone else to cover your job until you arrive. Everyone, for one reason or another, misses some time at work. If it isn't a regular problem, your employer can take care of the situation.

Remember, it is your responsibility to get to work on time. Situations beyond your control, such as a flat tire or a late bus may arise. However, forgetting to set your alarm clock the night before is not beyond your control.

Step two is to commit yourself to doing the best you can. Do your best work in the time allowed to complete the job. If you know the importance of your job, then you understand why it is important to do it right every time. With this kind of attitude, employers will know what to expect from you. Other employees will know they can depend on you to complete your job so they can complete theirs. Most people get annoyed if they have to redo someone else's work so that they can complete their own.

Commit yourself to doing your best work.

If you are given an assignment and don't fully understand what you are to do, ask questions. It is better to ask a question to clarify your assignment than to do the assignment incorrectly. Completing an assignment late because you didn't understand what you were to do is not a very good excuse for slowing down the entire company operation.

Some days you will think that just getting by is all right. You might think that no one will notice if you just put forth a minimal effort. Don't get caught in this trap. If all the employees in your company let this attitude affect their work, the overall quality of your product or service would be reduced to the minimum level. In today's business world, providing the minimum is not competitive. Everyday, companies that provide products or services of only minimal quality go out of business because their competition offers more.

Step three is to pace yourself and know your limitations. If you have a task to complete, be sure you have the time and the skill to complete it correctly. Sometimes employees accept or volunteer for more than they can handle. You are better off doing one job well and on time than two jobs poorly or late. An employer wants to know the job will be done. If you can't do the job correctly or on time, let your employer know so he or she can give you more time or adjust the assignment.

Some employees try to do more than they are able to impress the boss or fellow employees. Unfortunately, the end result may be that the job doesn't get done, or that it is done incorrectly. The overall company operation can be slowed down because one job was not done on time or correctly.

Remember the loan officers at the bank? If they tried to take on too much work and didn't pace themselves, the loan papers would not be ready for the customers when they arrive at the bank. When a customer has been promised the money to buy a shiny new car, they want the money! They don't want to hear excuses about why they will have to wait another day or two because the loan papers are not ready.

Step four is to *challenge* yourself. Challenge yourself to be the person on whom others can rely to do a good job. Think about what you are doing. Are you doing the best you can? Could you do anything to improve the quality of your work? Do others think of you when a job needs to be done reliably? Don't be afraid to get ideas from others on ways to improve the quality of your work. Reliability is an important strength for an employee to possess.

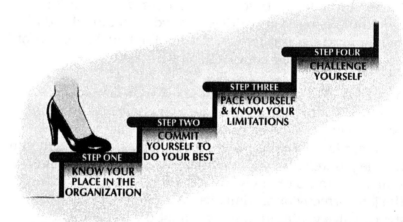

Take steps to establish a reputation for reliability.

Knowing Your Job

Some employees never learn their jobs very well. These people don't understand the importance of their jobs. Many jobs are a single step in a much longer process. If employees don't understand how their steps relate to the finished product, they don't understand their importance. You can learn the importance of your job by learning how it fits in the organization.

By understanding how your job fits in with the entire process, you will have a better idea why your job requires you to do the things you do. For example, consider this problem in an electronic manufacturing company:

Bob's job involved soldering several parts on a circuit board. His job was to solder one part in a certain direction on the circuit board. Because the part had a wire coming out of each end, Bob did not pay attention to the direction in which he placed the part onto the board. Sometimes the part was soldered right side up and sometimes upside down. Bob didn't see where the direction made any difference.

Some boards reached the next step of the manufacturing process with pieces soldered on backward. Workers in this part of the plant would have to fix the mistake because they couldn't complete their job with the part improperly soldered. This took extra time and slowed down the process.

If Bob had taken the time to see the entire operation; he would have understood why the part had to be placed on the board in a certain way.

In addition to learning the importance of your job, study the entire operation. This way you'll learn about the other jobs in your company. You may find that you would like to learn other jobs within the organization and expand your knowledge of the company's operations. Many companies are anxious to cross-train employees for other jobs. That way, if they need another employee to fill in on a job, they can use the employee who is trained for more than one job. Wouldn't it be nice to know your boss could depend on you in more than one area of the company?

Because competition is so fierce in today's businesses, many employers have realized the advantage of moving employees from department to department. For example, if the shipping department is experiencing a shortage of help, the boss can move a worker from another area to help shipping department personnel. This way, delivery schedules can be met and customers will remain satisfied with the company. It is to your advantage to be the employee who can be depended on to learn new jobs and fill temporary job openings.

There are other advantages to understanding the entire operation of your company. With such an understanding, you will be in a better position to see ways to make improvements in a product or service. If you do not see how your job relates to the rest of the company, it is not likely you will see a better way to do your job. Many companies encourage their employees to suggest ways to improve operations. Some of the most successful companies have built their success on employee's suggestions for improvement.

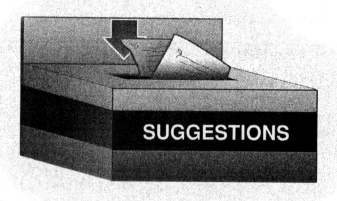

*Employees' suggestions can help
make a company successful.*

Learning your job so well that others look to you for help is one of the best ways to become important to your company. Be the expert in your area. It will pay off in the end. Take the initiative to learn your job well. Find out how your job fits into the entire process in your company. Look for ways to help your company improve its operation. You will enjoy your job more and your employer will see you as an important part of the operation.

Sharing the Credit

Employers are always looking for new ways to help their businesses succeed. A number of successful businesses now are using a technique called **peer-praising**. Employers using this technique hold weekly staff meetings in which the company's owner or manager encourages each employee to tell about something good a fellow worker has done. This prompts employees to look for the good things others are doing so they can share that information at staff meetings. Instead of finding fault with their peers, they are looking for the positive happenings in the company. Praising others creates a positive attitude that influences the entire operation.

You can create your own peer-praising program. Look for the good things your fellow workers are doing. Share your observations with others. If you have the opportunity, let someone's boss know about the good things his or her workers are doing. Looking for the good in others will help you maintain your positive attitude. When praising the work of others, you need to keep in mind that some people are not used to hearing compliments from their co-workers. They may think you are only trying to make points with your peers!

To avoid looking like you are on a campaign to find the good in everyone, you must develop subtle ways of sharing your information. Let's see how Shawn shared his observation with Karen's boss:

> Shawn was sitting next to Karen's boss, Art, at lunch. During a casual conversation, Shawn said to Art, "Yesterday we finished reorganizing the stockroom. I have to tell you, Karen was a lot of help. She drew up some rough plans for the reorganization that made things happen more easily than I ever imagined. She sure is a good organizer." Art agreed that Karen was a good worker.

If Shawn had simply walked up to Art and said, "Karen sure is organized, what a hard worker!" Art may have agreed with Shawn or he may have thought, "What was that all about?" By Shawn giving his reasons for praising Karen, it appeared much more sincere to Art. The most effective way to praise others is to be sincere. If you honestly mean what you're saying, your message can be very powerful. Those you work with will appreciate your extra efforts and you will feel good about yourself.

What about praising yourself? Is that bragging? Should you avoid telling others about yourself—especially if others are not doing it for you? What if your boss allows you to do a lot of work on your own? How is he or she going to know everything you have done? You must learn how to *blow your own horn*. Blowing your own horn means letting others know what you are doing. Just as praising others should be done subtly, you must be very careful how you praise yourself.

Self-praising is acceptable when it is done occasionally; but when it is done on a regular basis, it can be perceived as bragging. What a dilemma! You need to let your boss know what you are doing, yet you don't want to brag. How can you be subtle about praising yourself? In the previous example Shawn did just that. He praised himself in a very subtle way. Let's see how Shawn blew his own horn.

Shawn told Art about something he had done. He showed Art he was concerned about doing his job in an efficient manner. He also showed he was concerned about others. He did all this while talking about Karen! But Art wasn't his boss. What good did it do to tell Art? Shouldn't he have talked to his own boss? In this case, the opportunity was there to talk to Art. There was a very good chance that Art would talk to Shawn's boss about the positive comments Shawn made about Karen. If Shawn ends up working for Art someday, he will already have established a positive image of himself with Art. Do you see how looking for the positive in others can be helpful to you? Shawn didn't make those comments about Karen to help himself, he truly wanted to compliment her, but he helped himself at the same time.

If Shawn had said the same thing to his boss, she or he would have appreciated his positive comments about Karen. At the same time, his boss would have learned more about Shawn's positive attitude toward his job. Let's look at another way to blow your own horn without bragging about yourself:

Laurie had finished all her work early on Friday and had some time left before quitting for the day. She could have used this extra time on some simple little project or merely killed time until she could leave for home, but she didn't. With her extra time, she reorganized all the department files so she and the other workers could find information more quickly.

Laurie's boss is a very busy person and often doesn't know about all the extra work Laurie has done. Laurie realized that if she didn't let her boss know about her extra efforts, no one else would.

How could Laurie let her boss know she had taken the initiative and completed some work that needed to be done? Laurie could have said to her boss, "Mrs. Weber, I finished my work early on Friday, so I reorganized the department files. Now it is much easier for everyone to find information in those files." Laurie's boss would probably be impressed with Laurie's extra effort. However, if Laurie used this approach every week, or every time she did extra work, it would sound like bragging.

Blowing your own horn lets others know what you are doing.

Here is another way Laurie could let her boss know about her extra work. Laurie could have said, "Mrs. Weber, when I was reorganizing the files on Friday, I found these files that were completed several months ago. Should I send them to the warehouse for storage?" She also might have said, "Mrs. Weber, On Friday when I reorganized our files, I realized that the information in many of those files could be put in our computer and accessed more quickly. Do you see any problem with us computerizing those files?" In both examples, Laurie demonstrated what she had done but placed the emphasis of her discussion on a question, not herself. By asking a question, she showed her boss that she is interested in her job.

There is no single correct way to blow your own horn. One thing is sure, you can't do it the same way every time. You must look for opportunities to praise yourself. If you do it the same way each time, it is bragging. But, if you are subtle in your self-praise, you will let others know what you are doing without offending them.

Why should you blow your own horn? Employers rely on several sources of information to make their decisions regarding pay raises and promotions. For example, a supervisor may casually talk to other employees about the worker under consideration for advancement. He or she might also listen to comments others make about the employee. Often, a group of supervisors or managers will make the decision together. The group might discuss several employees and decide if a raise in pay is appropriate, or if they have the qualifications for a promotion.

If you are being considered for a raise or promotion, everyone who is a part of making that decision should know what kind of a worker you are and what you have done. It is to your benefit to be sure others know what you are doing. You can inform them of your efforts without bragging by blowing your own horn.

Success on the job requires that others know what
kind of work you do. Learn to blow your own horn.

Being a good employee involves more than just doing your job.
It includes knowing what your job is and how it fits into the
organization in which you work. It also means working well
with others and letting them know what you are doing for
the company. Make your work enjoyable by accepting the
challenge to be the best employee you can be.

Study Questions

1. In what ways can employees affect a business' success?

2. Name three ways of learning information quickly.

3. What is paraphrasing?

4. What are the four steps in creating a reputation for reliability?

5. Why is it important to know how your job fits into the organization?

6. How does peer-praising work? How can you use it to benefit yourself?

7. What does it mean to *blow your own horn*? Why should you do this only occasionally?

Chapter Five:
Setting Goals

Chapter Objectives

In this chapter you will:

1. Learn about the power of goal setting.

2. Explore ways to use goal setting for personal success.

3. Learn to develop the habit of goal setting and planning.

4. Identify the pressures that can prevent you from planning and goal setting.

5. Practice the steps of successful goal setting.

6. Begin to develop ways of using goal setting to be successful on the job.

If you have a goal in life that takes a lot of energy,
that requires a lot of work, that incurs a great deal
of interest and that is a challenge to you, you will
always look forward to waking up to see what the
new day brings.

Susan Polis Schultz
American poet

Goals—Powerful Tools

In 1989, a small school in southern Oregon won the state
football championship. The entire community was excited
and very proud of the team and its coaches. They even had
a parade to celebrate the victory. Why would a community
get so excited by a football victory? After all, teams win state
championships all the time.

The community, the school, and the players were excited
because this very small school had never before won a state
football championship. In fact, this school was celebrating its
100th anniversary and had never even gone to the state football play-offs until two years before winning the championship.

Over the years, the larger schools in the conference domina-
ted league play. These schools had twice as many students
to choose from when teams were being organized. The small
southern Oregon school just hadn't been able to compete with
these big schools. The athletes worked hard each year, but
the other teams always had more talent.

When the final play-off game was over, sports writers, coaches, and football fans could hardly believe a team from a small rural school had defeated the biggest and best in the state. Everyone was amazed at their undefeated season and the state championship—everyone, that is, except the players and the coaches. They knew they could win all their league games and prove they were the best in the state. Why were they so sure they could win? To answer this question, we must learn more about this special team.

When the players on this championship team were in the eighth grade, the new high school football coach came to them with a proposal. At a meeting with these young players, he asked them if they would like to win in their league and go to the state football championship when they reached high school. This was a very bold proposal for the coach to make because the team had never won the league title, let alone gone to the state championship!

The coach went on to tell the players that they could win the league title in high school if they set a **goal** for themselves and worked very hard to reach that goal. But there was more to the coach's plan than just setting a goal. He told the team that each member would have to set an individual goal to develop strength and athletic skill to help the team reach a goal of winning the league title. Each player would have to dedicate himself and make a commitment to reach his individual goal.

As time passed, the coach worked with each player to develop their goals. They worked on a written plan of action that would help the players improve. They learned that it is much easier to say you are going to do something than it is to write it down and stick to the plan. Some of the players had good intentions, but found it easier to skip the steps they had in their plans. However, most of the players worked hard and stayed with the plan of action.

As these young athletes entered high school, their efforts began to pay off; the team won most of its games. Because the players had set a team goal, they worked well together. Players improved each season until they won the league title and went on to compete in the state play-offs.

During the second round of the state play-offs, they lost and were eliminated from the competition. After the game, the coach congratulated the players for reaching their goal of playing in the state play-offs. He then asked the players what their next goal would be. Without hesitation, they said they wanted to win the state championship. The coach told them they would have to set new individual goals and work toward the team goal of winning the state championship.

The next year, the team won each league game with very little difficulty. Only two of the largest schools posed much of a problem for this team with a mission beyond the weekly games.

Undefeated, they went on to the state play-offs. Although the team received little attention in the sports pages, one by one they won each of their play-off games. Finally, the competition narrowed to only two teams. When the game ended, the team from the little high school had reached its long awaited goal. People shook their heads in disbelief. How could this happen?

The only ones who really knew how it happened were in the locker room celebrating their victory and the achievement of a goal set when they were in the eighth grade.

Today these high school athletes talk about the excitement of winning a state football championship. They also talk about the power of goal setting.

Goals are powerful tools.

People talk about their goals every day. They plan to lose weight, quit smoking, read a book, fix the car, etc. So if goal setting is so effective, why do people always talk about goals, but never seem to achieve them? The answer to that question is the key to successful goal setting.

The Anatomy of a Goal

Thomas Edison said, "Show me a thoroughly satisfied man and I will show you a failure." What kind of a statement is that? How can you be a failure if you are satisfied? Edison, of course, was a very successful person. His inventions are used by millions of people around the world. Presidents invited him to meet world leaders, and he was asked to speak at colleges and business conferences. Thomas Edison truly was famous.

Was he satisfied? Of course not. Sure, he was very successful, but to Edison there was always another challenge in life—
another invention to be made. If Edison had been satisfied
with his first or second invention, would he have gone on to
develop hundreds of other inventions?

Edison had both long-term and short-term goals. His short-
term goals were steps to his long-term goals. When Edison
was able to use electricity to cause a wire to glow, he had
made a major breakthrough in the development of the electric
light. The fact that it would only last a short time before
burning out was not important at that point. Edison had
reached a short-term goal. However, his long-term goal was
to develop an electric light that could be used for long periods
of time to light large areas. Eventually he developed a light
bulb that was so effective, it was first used to light baseball
fields for night games. When Edison did that, he had reached
his long-term goal. What do you think he did next? He set
new goals for himself—he wasn't satisfied.

If you study the lives of successful people, you will find most
of them have one thing in common; they set goals and work
at achieving them. Does that surprise you? It shouldn't. In
order to be successful, you must determine what needs to be
done and develop a plan to get there.

Successful people—world leaders, doctors, actors, Olympic
athletes, teachers, astronauts, race car drivers, company
presidents, musicians, etc.—have learned the secret of goal
setting. These men and women know they must set goals for
themselves and work to achieve those goals. We can use the
same techniques to help us be successful on the job and in
everything we do in life.

People who talk about setting goals to lose weight, stop smoking, save money, etc. have the right idea, but often, they are not *committed* to their goals. These people *talk* about what they want, but they do not *do* anything to make it happen! How can *YOU* make things happen through goal setting?

To understand goal setting, you must understand why most people are not successful at it. Setting a goal is a **commitment** to **accomplish** something. Commitment means you truly want to achieve something and will do your very best at working toward that **achievement**. So why is it so difficult to set a goal and achieve it? The answer to that is the *fear of failure*. People often do not set goals because they are afraid they might fail to reach them. It is easier to not set a goal or to set one and not work toward it, than to try your hardest and fail. After all, you can't fail to achieve a goal that you do not have. Or, if you set the goal and do not really work toward its achievement, you can always tell yourself, "Well I could have reached it, but I didn't really try!"

The person who sets a goal to get an "A" on a test and then doesn't study hard to prepare for it, hasn't consciously decided not to reach the goal; he or she has unconsciously avoided the possibility of failure to reach the goal by not making a commitment. There was no *real* commitment, therefore, in that person's mind he or she hasn't failed. It's a good thing Thomas Edison didn't have that attitude—we might still be using candles for reading lights!

Developing well-defined goals and committing to them is the secret to good goal setting. Developing and achieving goals is hard work, but the results can be amazing. Let's look at another person who used goals to succeed...

"Shelly Mann could scarcely move a muscle, much less stand. Stricken with polio at the age of five, Shelly began going to a swimming pool to get strength back into her weak arms and legs. She cried tears of joy the day she was able to lift an arm out of the water—a major triumph. Her first goal was to swim the width of the pool, then the length. As she reached each goal, she set a new one." (*The Edge: the Guide to Fulfilling Dreams, Maximizing Success and Enjoying a Lifetime of Achievement*, [Cleveland, OH: Getting the Edge Company, 1990] 2-9)

In the 1956 Olympics, Shelly Mann won the 100 meter butterfly event. She held the world record in all 100 and 200 meter butterfly events. This young woman who set goals for herself, is one of the greats among American female swimmers.

Here are the steps involved in setting goals:

1. Clearly define your goal.

2. Determine the obstacles that stand in the way of reaching your goal.

3. Identify ways to overcome those obstacles.

4. Describe the rewards you will receive if you reach your goal.

5. Develop positive affirmations about reaching your goal.

6. Find or create visual representations of your potential success.

Defining Your Goal

It is very important that you clearly understand what you wish to achieve. Many people set goals that are not clearly defined. If a goal is not clearly defined, you do not have a clear target on which to set your sights. Losing weight is a good example. Simply setting a goal of losing weight is not specific enough. How much weight do you want to lose? By what date do you want to lose it? If you lose ten pounds in a year will you have you reached your goal? You must be very specific about what you wish to accomplish.

Here is a better way of describing a goal to lose weight: Decide to lose five pounds in five weeks. This way, you can measure your progress and have a feeling of success. Each week when you weigh yourself, you can see your progress. Maybe you will shed one pound per week, giving yourself a feeling of success each week. Had your goal been simply to lose five pounds with no time limits, you would weigh yourself each week without a true sense of success because the scale would tell you the full five pounds had not yet been lost.

A clear description of your goal becomes even more important when you set more difficult goals for yourself. What if you were trying to lose twenty-five pounds? Each day you would weigh yourself and the scale would indicate you have not lost twenty-five pounds. After a few days of this lack of success, it would be easy to decide this is just too much of a challenge and give up. On the other hand, if your goal was to lose twenty-five pounds in five months, you could break that long-term goal down into a short-term goal of five pounds per month. To make it even easier, you could establish a short-term goal of losing one and a quarter pounds per week. Does it sound a little easier to lose a pound and a quarter per week instead of twenty-five pounds in no particular time frame? You bet it does! That is the power of goal setting. You know what you want and you have a plan to get there.

How about a new car? Would you like to have a new car?
How would you describe the goal to get a new car? You could
simply say, "I will get a new car," but what is missing from
that goal? What kind of car do you want and how much does
it cost? When will you reach your goal? How will you measure your progress toward reaching your goal? In order to buy
a new car you will have to save money for a down payment.
Unless you have lots of money, you will have to borrow the
rest of the money to pay for your new car. What will your
payments be on the loan? Can you afford those payments?
These are all questions you must ask yourself as you establish
your goal to buy a new car.

Can you define your goal?

Identifying Obstacles

The power of goal setting is in the establishment of a plan
to reach your goal. Most people spend a minimal amount of
time planning their personal lives, but successful people know
where they want to go and have a plan to get there. When a
problem is encountered, they usually have a plan to deal with
that problem. It is no wonder people who set goals seem so
confident about their ability to achieve their goals.

How can you have a plan for dealing with problems that may
interfere with reaching your goal? The second step in goal
setting is to identify **obstacles** that you may encounter as you
work toward your goal. What problems might you encounter
in buying a new car? The down payment could be a real
problem for many people. Monthly payments also could be
a problem. How can you overcome these obstacles?

The first step in the process would be a short-term goal to
learn about the cars in which you would be interested and
how much they would cost. What kind of gas mileage do they
get, and what is their history for repair costs? Next would
be a short-term goal of learning as much as you can about
financing a car. How much money will be needed for a down
payment? What are the interest rates, monthly payments,
insurance costs, licensing fees, etc.?

As you gather more information, you will begin to identify the
problems you may encounter. You may not have enough
money for a down payment. The monthly payments might be
a little more than you can afford. Gas mileage might not be as
good as your current car, which would increase your gasoline
costs. Insurance on a new car will cost more than on an old
car. These are all obstacles. If you walk into the showroom
without a plan for buying a new car and encounter all these

obstacles, chances are you will walk out believing a new car is
for others, but not for you—you can't afford it. However, with
a plan of action that **anticipates** these obstacles, you may
drive that new car home.

Remember, we identified two short-term goals to help you
reach your long-term goal of owning a new car. First, learn
about the car and its costs. Second, learn about financing
and purchasing costs. Now let's see how you can overcome
the obstacles by setting some additional short-term goals.

    A. You do not have enough money for a
       down payment.

You will need another $1000 to make the full down payment.
Can you save your money until you have the additional
$1000? If so, how long will it take and how much money
must you save each week? Your third short-term goal might
be to save $50 a week for five months. At the end of five
months you will have an extra $1000 for your down payment.

    B. The monthly payments are too high.

Postponing your purchase might be one way to deal with
payments that are too high. Dealers and manufacturers will
be anxious to sell last year's models to make room for new
models that are being delivered. Rebates and discounts will
be offered to buyers of last year's models. Even though they
are last year's models, they are still new cars. Also, if you wait
to purchase your car, you will have more time to increase your
down payment, which will help lower your monthly payments.
Another possibility would be to purchase a used car that
has low mileage.

Short-term goal number four might be to determine the best
time and way for you to buy a car that will meet your monthly
payment requirements.

C. Insurance and gas expenses will increase.

As you try to think of a way to overcome the additional
expenses you may encounter for gas, compare your old car
to the new one you are considering. What is the advantage
of the new car over the old? Is it more comfortable, quieter,
or more reliable? How much are you spending on repairs?
Could you save enough money on repairs to offset the additional insurance costs? Is there a model that gets better gas
mileage than your current car? Are there changes in your
insurance coverage that might lower your costs, such as
raising your **deductible** or making semi-annual payments
instead of monthly payments? Your fifth goal might involve
calculating the repair and insurance costs on your old car,
and looking for new car models that get better gas mileage
and have a history of low repair costs.

Each short-term goal should be clearly written down with a
time schedule as a way to measure progress. Setting goals is
a personal process. Each person will have a different set of
short-term goals to reach their long-term goals. The above
examples would not necessarily be the same for everyone.

To recap, if you have a long-term goal of owning a new car, we
identified five short-term goals that might help you reach that
long-term goal. As the short-term goals are reached, more
information is provided to help define the long-term goal.
Finally, a long-term goal is identified that lists several cars
that could be purchased, the steps necessary to purchase a
car, and a date by which the goal will be reached. By using
short-term goals, you would increase your chances of driving
home a new car—maybe not tomorrow, but sometime in the
near future.

Identifying Your Rewards

Once you have established a plan to reach a long-term goal, you must **motivate** yourself to reach this goal. One method of motivating yourself is to describe the rewards you will receive if your goal is achieved. Identifying your rewards is like learning how much you will be paid for work performed. Would you work for free? Probably not. Reaching goals works the same way. If there is no reward, you are not likely to work very hard to achieve your goal. If you establish a goal and cannot determine what your rewards will be, you probably need to reevaluate your goal or set another. You are kidding yourself if you think you will work for nothing.

The two long-term goals we have talked about were losing weight and owning a new car. What rewards do you see in accomplishing these goals? The rewards for losing weight might be better health, improved **self-esteem**, or improved appearance. Each person may have different rewards for the same goal. Goal setting is very personal.

The rewards of owning a new car might include a sense of accomplishment and success, pride in your new car, relief from worries that your old car will breakdown, or the ability to take a trip in comfort. Again, there can be many others. The important thing to remember is the value of knowing and reviewing your rewards on a regular basis.

Reviewing the rewards or motivations for your goals is just as important as reviewing the goals themselves. Can you imagine how difficult it would be to go to work everyday if you were only paid every six months? After a few weeks you would begin to lose interest in your work. Reviewing your rewards for goal setting keeps you working toward those goals. Goals and rewards should be reviewed at least once a week, if not daily. There is a direct correlation between how often you review goals and rewards and your success at achieving those goals. Dr. Martin Luther King Jr. used the phrase, "Keep your eye on the prize." Your prize is achieving your goal and enjoying its rewards. *Keep your eye on the prize!*

Making Positive Affirmations

As you work toward your goals, some people and situations will make it difficult to stick to your plan for reaching your goal. Some people will tell you that you cannot reach your goal. They might say:

> A new car? Why the cost of new cars is out of sight! How can you consider buying a new car on your salary?

> Lose twenty-five pounds? I have tried seven times to lose just fifteen; after the first ten pounds it's impossible.

How do you deal with negative comments? The secret is in making positive **affirmations** — statements that support your efforts.

Positive affirmations remind you that you have developed a plan and that you will succeed. Here are some positive affirmations related to the goals of a new car and weight loss.

- I have a plan to lose twenty-five pounds and know I am strong enough to reach my goal.

- When I reach my goal of losing twenty-five pounds I will feel and look better than I have in ten years.

- I am in control of my body. I will not be controlled by food commercials or food that is offered to me that I don't need.

- By developing a plan to buy a new car, I have made one of many future steps toward improving my personal situation.

- I have worked hard and deserve to reward myself with a new car.

- I know the problems involved with the purchase of a new car and I know how to overcome them.

Positive affirmations, when reviewed daily, can help you overcome those around you who will try to sidetrack you with their negative comments. You must maintain a positive attitude and believe you can reach your goals. If you get lazy and do not review your goals, rewards, and positive affirmations, negative influences will reduce your self-confidence.

Visualizing Your Goal

Visualizing your goal is another way of reinforcing your determination to succeed. You can create powerful *goal reminders* for yourself by cutting out or drawing pictures that represent your goal. For example, every morning as you brush your teeth you see a picture taped to your mirror—a picture of a shiny new car like the one you want to buy. Later in the day you might be tempted to give up your goal. A new stereo system might catch your eye, and the salesperson tells you it can be yours for only $100 per month. But that's as much as you are saving for your car! You remember the picture taped to your mirror, and decide not to buy the stereo. That fresh vision of the new car made it easier to turn down the stereo— even though it may be a year before you can get the new car. Can you see the sun shining on that new paint? Can you hear the purr of that engine? Can you smell the new interior of your car? Visualizing your goal reinforces your commitment to succeed by using all of your senses.

If you put a picture of someone who looks trim and healthy on your refrigerator door, it is easier to take an apple out of that refrigerator instead of a dish of ice cream. Can you see yourself effortlessly skiing down the slope, feeling strong and healthy as you twist and turn? Can you feel the warm rays of the sun as you lay on the beach, not feeling uncomfortable in a bathing suit? This is the power of visualization. Cut out or draw pictures that remind yourself of the rewards you will receive when you reach your goal. Look at them daily and let your senses reinforce your desire to succeed.

Visualize your goal!

Developing a Plan for Success

Identifying a goal and the steps necessary to achieve your goal is the most difficult part of goal setting. The final step is to develop a plan that outlines all your goals. With a plan that identifies your goals, you gain control over your life. Instead of waiting for things to happen, you will *make* things happen. By setting goals and working toward them, *YOU* will be in control. Organization of your goals is called a *plan for success*.

To reach the greatest level of success in goal setting, you must *write them down and review them regularly*. The following page illustrates the structure for your plan for success.

Plan for Success

Long-term Goals: _____

_____

_____

_____

_____

Short-term Goals: _____

_____

_____

_____

_____

Obstacles: _____

_____

_____

_____

_____

Rewards: _____

_____

_____

_____

_____

Positive Affirmations: _____

_____

_____

_____

Pictures to Support Your Goals:

Comments: _____

_____

_____

_____

_____

_____

_____

Dates Plan Reviewed: _____

_____

_____

Review your plan for success daily. Read your goals and review the rewards associated with them. Read your positive affirmations and study the pictures that support your goals. Record the date each time you do this. As time goes on, you will develop the habit of dealing with situations in an organized manner. As you reach your goals, set new goals. Don't be satisfied with reaching a goal—stretch yourself and discover you can do more.

Employers will tell you that people who know where they are going and how to get there make the best employees. An employer wants an employee who can make decisions and get the job done. By setting goals in your personal life, you are better able to deal with personal problems. If you can deal with your personal problems, you are less likely to bring those problems to work. Employers like that. Today's world requires more of employees. There is less room for **distractions** in the workplace. Goal setting will help you become the decisive employee you would like to be. Develop the habit of goal setting now and begin to discover your true potential.

Reggie Jackson had a tremendous career in professional baseball. He once described the power of goal setting in this way: "True success is one of our greatest needs." (*The Edge: the Guide to Fulfilling Dreams, Maximizing Success and Enjoying a Lifetime of Achievement*, [Cleveland, OH: Getting the Edge Company, 1990] 2-27) He went on to say that success is not something you stumble onto or find by accident. It is something for which you must sincerely prepare. Take a good look at successful people, he continued, and you will see the same consistent qualities every time—qualities in one's character that make one strive for a goal with a standard of unmatched excellence.

Study Questions

1. What is the difference between a short-term goal and a long-term goal?

2. What are you doing when you set a goal?

3. What do most successful people have in common with each other?

4. What makes it difficult to set and achieve goals?

5. Name the six steps involved in setting goals.

6. Why is it important to clearly define your goals?

7. How can identifying obstacles help you plan for success?

8. Why should you identify the rewards you will receive when your goal is reached?

9. Describe, in your own words, how positive affirmations can help you reach your goals.

Chapter Six:

Understanding the Organization

Chapter Objectives

In this chapter you will:

1. Learn about the importance of knowing how your company works, as well as the products and services it provides.

2. Find ways to determine how information is communicated in your company and how to use that system to your benefit.

3. Begin to develop a plan to learn as much about your company as possible.

4. Learn how to develop systems, relationships, and contacts that will help you on the job.

5. See how working successfully within your company will provide long-term benefits.

*Every company has two organizational structures:
The formal one is written on the charts; the other is
the everyday relationship of men and women in the
organization.*

> Harold S. Geneen
> Former Chairman,
> International Telephone and Telegraph

Learning About Your Company

Every organization has employees who work at a variety of
tasks to provide goods and services. In the past, most jobs
required workers to do the same job over and over. Today,
companies are using employees for many jobs within the
organization. This way, the employer can move an employee
to the job where they are most needed. This change in the
use of employees creates new challenges and opportunities for
today's workers. To take advantage of these opportunities,
you must learn as much as possible about the company, the
jobs, and the employees within that company.

How is Your Company Organized?

The complexity of a company will vary depending on its size
and type of business. If you work for a small retail store,
there may only be three or four employees in your company.
On the other hand, if you work for a major corporation, there
may be hundreds or even thousands of employees within the
organization, making the structure complex. Regardless
of the size of your company, it is important to understand
why your job is important to the organization.

One of the first steps toward understanding your company is to find out about its history—how it started and how it became the company for which you now work. Talk to other employees about the company. Let them know you are new and interested in learning about the company. Keep in mind, however, that some employees may not care about the company and know little about it. If you encounter an employee like this, don't **overreact** to his or her lack of interest. Just thank the person for whatever information he or she may have provided and change the subject. Some employees are only concerned about *their* job. If you act too anxious to learn about your new job or the company, they may feel threatened by your actions. Be sensitive to this situation. You can talk to other employees who may be more interested in their job and the company.

Your boss can be another good source of information. Usually a person who has been promoted to a management position has worked at several jobs within the company and has been with the company for awhile. Also, they are interested in their work and their company. You may find that your boss will be very anxious to share his or her experience with you. Your boss may find it refreshing to talk to an enthusiastic worker. Not all employees show a lot of interest in the company for which they work. Many workers are satisfied to just do their job and collect their paychecks. You have an opportunity to share a higher level of interest with your boss and co-workers.

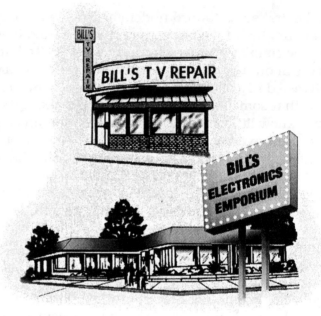

Learn the history of your company.

As you learn more about the company, you will begin to see the direction the company has taken or will be taking. This is valuable information because it can show you how you and your job fit within the company. It can also show you what opportunities may be available to you in the future.

Knowledge of your company, its employees, and the jobs within that company is a very powerful tool for personal success. You need to learn about the organization. Who makes the decisions? Where has the company been and where is it going? Armed with the tool of knowledge, you can develop a plan for success within the organization.

The Chain of Command

To function efficiently, an organization must have a plan for making decisions and a system of communication. This plan is called the **chain of command**. In a typical chain of command, the president of the company makes a decision and tells the vice president. The vice president tells the general manager and the general manager tells the superintendent. The superintendent tells the foreman about the decision, and the foreman tells the workers. Does this sound complicated? Sometimes it can be a real problem getting the message all the way to the bottom of the chain. If you think of a pyramid, the president would be at the top and the workers at the bottom. In between would be different layers of management. Directions usually go from top to bottom. The result of that information, or **feedback**, goes from the bottom to the top.

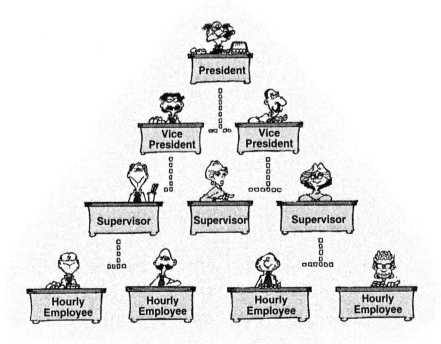

The chain of command.

Here is an example of how the chain of command might work. The president of ABC Soft Drink Company wants to increase company production by 200 cases of soda pop per day. She talks to her vice presidents about increasing production. They all agree that working one hour overtime each day will allow the company to meet the new production schedule. The vice president in charge of manufacturing sends a memo to the production manager who is responsible for production within the company. The production manager sends a memo to the manager who oversees the manufacturing and bottling of the soda. He also notifies the person in charge of distribution. Furthermore, a memo must be sent to the person who orders the ingredients for the pop and the empty bottles that will be filled with pop. In this way, everyone involved with producing the soda knows about the new plans.

While the production manager is dealing with the manufacturing plant, the vice president in charge of operations must send notices to the personnel, payroll, accounting, and marketing departments. Managers in each department will explain the new production schedule to their employees. The Payroll Department will notify Accounting of the increased wages and benefits the employees will receive. Marketing will notify distributors of the increased availability of the product.

Once all the departments are notified, the reverse process takes place. As more information is learned about the effects of increased production, workers tell supervisors, and supervisors tell managers. Managers notify vice presidents, etc. as the information continues up the chain of command.

As an employee, you need to understand the chain of command. One of the messages that travels this line of communication is information about opportunities for advancement. When a person leaves the company or a new job is created, the personnel office notifies the department manager who, in turn, notifies the various supervisors.

Sometimes the message goes the other way. You may tell your supervisor that you are interested in transferring to another department. You expect that information to be passed on the supervisor in the other department, or possibly to the personnel office. Why do you need to understand the chain of command if all this information is going to automatically move through the communication system? Because the chain often has a weak link.

What is a weak link? Sometimes managers and supervisors don't communicate very well. Sometimes supervisors don't communicate very well with their workers. Do you see the weak links? If your supervisor doesn't receive all the information from his or her boss, how can your supervisor pass it on to you? Maybe your supervisor gets the information and is not very good about passing it on to his or her employees. What about the message you want sent up the chain of command? Will the supervisor in the department that interests you know about your desire to transfer? The information you receive or pass on is only as good as the line of communication within your company.

Failure to communicate is not necessarily intentional. Lack of communication may result from work overload or from carelessness at some level of management. For example, if the department manager has just been given a major project to complete in a short period of time, he or she might skip the meeting in which relevant information was discussed. Perhaps he or she went to the meeting, but didn't bother to pass the information on to the next level. Some managers just are not good communicators, and may unintentionally change the facts when they relay the information.

Do you remember playing a game in school where everyone lined up to pass along a message? The first person in line told the second person some information, then that person told the next person, and so on. After the last person was given the message, he or she repeated the message so everyone could hear it. What happened? The message the last person heard was different from that told by the first person. The chain of command in a company can be like that line of people sharing messages.

As an employee who needs accurate information, you need to find a way to get the right message. By understanding your company's chain of command, you can determine how to be in the middle of that line of messages instead of at the end.

The first step in learning about the lines of communication in your company is to talk to other workers. Employees who have been around a while know who the good communicators are. Some supervisors will communicate a lot of information to their employees and others may not. Listen to the conversations of other workers. If you hear something that should be general knowledge to everyone but that you have not heard before, you may have discovered a weak link in the line of communication. You will have to find a way to get around this problem.

If your boss is not passing on information to you, you will need to develop a good relationship with a supervisor or a trusted employee in another department. This may sound like a sneaky thing to do, but it isn't. You are merely getting to know other people in your company so you have the greatest opportunity to learn about what is happening where you work. Knowing other people who have a good line of communication with upper management is even more important if you want to send information up the chain of command. Keep in mind that the way you approach others to avoid the weak link is very important.

To understand the process of expanding your communication base, let's look at an example of how Marilyn conveyed her interest in a promotion to upper management.

Marilyn had worked very hard for two years in the payroll office. She attended classes at night to earn a bookkeeping certificate. Now she wanted to be considered for a possible opening in the accounts payable department, but her boss, Jim, didn't communicate very well with his employees. He tended to discourage them from moving to another position within the company because he didn't want to be bothered with finding a replacement after they left. Marilyn had casually mentioned to Jim that she had heard the accounting department needed an accounts payable clerk and she felt her newly learned skills would be useful in that position. Jim's only reply was that his department was working well and Marilyn probably wouldn't be happy in another department.

Marilyn decided the only way she was going to have an opportunity for a position in accounting was to let the accounting supervisor know of her interest in the job. She tried to think of a way to get her message to the other supervisor. Marilyn decided she would work through her friend in the accounting department. The next day while on her break, she visited her friend Jan. Jan had a good relationship with her boss. They decided Jan would casually mention to her boss about Marilyn's interest in the job and her recently earned certificate. That would open the door for further discussion about Marilyn's interest in the job.

The next day Jan's boss, Margaret, stopped at her desk to see how she was doing on a weekly report. Jan told Margaret that she had a friend who was very interested in the accounts payable position. She went on to say her friend had gone to school at night to gain the skills she needed for that job. Jan asked her boss if she thought Marilyn would have a chance at the job and if so, how she would go about applying for it. Margaret said she was very interested in talking to Marilyn. She suggested that Marilyn fill out the necessary papers and submit them to the personnel office through her supervisor.

Jan knew this might be a problem. She didn't know if Marilyn's supervisor would send the forms to personnel, and if he did, he probably would not be very supportive of Marilyn's move. She told Marilyn about her conversation with her boss.

Marilyn filled out the necessary papers and gave them to her boss. She mentioned to him that she felt the new position would allow her to grow personally and use the new skills she had acquired. Jim said he would pass the request on the personnel office. Jim didn't seem mad, but he didn't show much enthusiasm for the idea either.

Marilyn and Jan discussed the situation and decided Jim might be slow in forwarding the request to personnel. To assure that Marilyn's request was reviewed by her boss, Jan would ask her boss if she had seen Marilyn's request. They agreed Jan should wait three days before talking to her boss.

Jan asked her boss if she had received Marilyn's application for the accounts receivable position. Margaret told her she hadn't received the paperwork and asked Jan for the name of Marilyn's supervisor. When Jan said it was Jim, her boss smiled and said she knew why she hadn't seen the paperwork. Margaret told Jan she would talk to Jim about the it. Jan asked her if she thought Jim would be upset with Marilyn. Margaret replied that she had worked with Jim for some time and knew how to handle the situation. A week later Marilyn was promoted to the new position in the accounting department.

Marilyn had discovered a weak link in the chain of command. She found a way to get around it and accomplish her goal. Marilyn was lucky Margaret knew Jim was not supportive of employees who wanted to leave his department. Margaret knew how to handle the situation.

Had Margaret not known Jim, Marilyn would have had to find a way to let Margaret know about the problem with Jim. Every situation will be different. A smart employee will find a way to deal with new situations as they arise. Knowing your company's chain of command and how it works is part of being successful on the job.

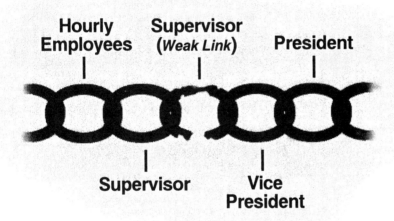

Is there a weak link in your company's chain of command?

Formal Chains of Command and Informal Chains of Command

As you can see, the system for communication within a company is only as effective as the people involved in that system. If a company is small and the people in the chain of command are good communicators, then the system works well. The bigger the company is, the more opportunities there are for a breakdown in the information sharing process. It is up to you to evaluate your company's system and find ways to deal with any problems that may exist within that system.

Because communication can be more difficult in larger organizations, the communication problems are usually handled by an **informal chain of command**. The employees already have found the weak links and worked around those problem areas. You may not have to figure out your own system for dealing with weak links in the chain; one may already exist. Good managers know who their good employees are and they listen to them. They also know which managers are good communicators and which ones are not. A manager who respects the abilities of his or her secretary may listen more carefully to him or her than some other supervisor.

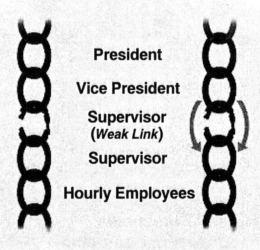

President

Vice President

Supervisor
(*Weak Link*)

Supervisor

Hourly Employees

**Formal Chain   Informal Chain
of Command   of Command**

*Can you identify an informal
chain of command in your company?*

In the previous example, Margaret knew Jim's strengths and weakness. When she realized Jim was Marilyn's supervisor, she knew she had to deal with the situation differently than under the normal chain of command. She also knew Jan was a good employee and wouldn't recommend Marilyn if she didn't believe she was qualified. Marilyn and Jan were not trying to deceive Jim; they were just trying to deal with a communication problem. Margaret was not trying to upstage Jim, she understood the problem and worked with Marilyn and Jan to solve the problem. This working arrangement between employees and managers goes on in many organizations.

Be careful; if you suspect there is a problem, make sure the problem has to do with poor communication and not poor performance. If you apply for a promotion or job change and your supervisor explains that you are not qualified, weigh that information carefully. It would be easy to tell yourself that your boss doesn't realize your potential and try to go around him or her. This could create even more problems for you. Employee promotions and transfers usually involve the approval of several managers. Those managers respect each other's **authority** and may not react in a positive way if you try to go around your boss and speak directly to them.

If you have trouble getting company information on time or passing information up the chain of command, look for ways to get around the problem. If you have a problem with your boss that is not related to communication, you will need to find another way to deal with your problem. In the following chapters, you will learn other ways to deal with the challenges of being successful on the job.

Just as you learned the history of the company by listening to others, you can also learn about an informal chain of command. Those who have worked at the company for some time, will know how to work within the system. Be careful not to confuse gossip with information about the weak links in the company communication system. An employee who complains about a supervisor may be dealing with a personal issue. The employee may **infer** that another supervisor would have been more **responsive**. This may or may not be true. File this information away and don't act on it until you get more data to support the facts. If you hear the same information from others, there may be some truth in what you are hearing. The best way to confirm this information is to watch what goes on regarding the chain of command. You may find that the comments of other employees are accurate. On the other hand, you may find that an employee has a problem and is blaming someone else for it. At least you have some information to use as you learn about the lines of communication within the company.

As you gather information you will begin to separate facts from gossip. You will identify the employees you can believe and those who are just complaining. Watching the interaction between employees and supervisors will help you understand how information flows within your company. The most important thing to remember is that there may be an informal chain of command within your company. Your job is to determine if the system exists and how to use it for your benefit without threatening your fellow workers and supervisor. Ask questions, listen carefully, gather information, and learn about lines of communication within your company.

Developing Your Own Communication Network

A chain of command, either informal or formal, is only one way to gain information about what is going on within a company. Successful employees learn to develop other sources of information. The following is a list of four other ways to gather information about the company.

1. **Visit other departments in the company.** Many workers make the mistake of not knowing what is going on in other parts of their company. Talk to the workers you meet to find out about them and their work. Meet their supervisors and introduce yourself. Develop friendly relationships that will encourage them to discuss the company, their department, and themselves. Be sincere and honest with them. You should be interested in these people and their jobs because you want to learn, not because you want to use them.

2. **Identify the movers and shakers.** In every company there are individuals who think positively, work hard, and get things done. Meet these people and develop a working relationship with them. They may be fellow workers or managers at different levels. These people are the center of action. You may be able to help them and they may help you. Movers and shakers can provide you with information about job openings and changes in the company. Furthermore, their attitude is contagious—you might become one of them!

3. **Develop contacts at all levels within the company.** Integrate yourself vertically and horizontally within the organization. In other words, know people on your level as well as those above and below you. It doesn't hurt to know your boss' supervisor or the new employee at the lowest level in the company. Don't get caught in the trap of only associating with the few people around you, get to know lots of people. You will be surprised how interesting other people and their jobs can be.

4. **Don't be afraid to help others.** In addition to meeting and talking to people, you should help others when you can. For example, if you are visiting with someone in another department and they need a report but can't leave their desk, volunteer to get it for them. This will

improve your working relationship, and someday they might be able to help you. Of course, you shouldn't help someone just so they owe you. Help people because you want to help them. If they help you at a later time, that's just an added benefit.

Because you know a number of people at all levels in the company, you will find yourself providing information about the company that will be helpful to others. For example, a fellow worker may need to solve a problem and not know where to go for information. With your knowledge of the company, you may not only be able to tell them which department to call, but who to speak to in that department. Maintaining a positive attitude and helping others will make you feel good. It also can help you learn more about your company.

Develop your own communication network.

You can work very hard for years in a company and still be overlooked when new jobs open simply because you do not have your own communication network. As we mentioned previously, blowing your own horn is one way of not being overlooked. To do this, however, you must know the people involved. In other words, you must know *TO WHOM* you should blow your own horn. That way, when you accomplish something important you will have a system to let others know what you have done. Talk to those around you, and know what is going on in your company. Use your personal communication network.

Know Your Company's Products and Services

It's amazing how many people know very little about the products and services their company provides. Some people work for a company for years and never bother to really *know* their company. Part of knowing your company is to know why it is in business. The job you are doing in your company is only part of the process. To understand the entire process, you must know about the end product or service.

When a magazine is printed, it is printed in several steps. Blues, reds, yellows, and greens are combined to make a color picture. When a page is printed with a color picture, each color is printed separately. First, a page is printed in one color. For example, the reds may be printed first and allowed to dry. Then the same page is run through the printing process again, only this time blues may be printed. As each color is printed, the picture begins to look like the one taken by the photographer. Each color run affects the final product.

If you worked for a printer and your job was to run a printing press, it would be easy just to do your job and not worry about the final product. However, by not knowing how your work affects the final product, you would be unable to find ways to do your job better and improve the finished product. Perhaps you are printing a page that has only blue ink, and another person runs the press that prints the reds. It would be important for you to look at the finished page to get a better understanding of the process. By doing this, you may even realize it would be better to print the colors in a different order, or change the way the press is set up.

Your employer may only expect you to run the printing press. You can take on the responsibility to learn about the finished product—and possible ways to improve that product. Each company is different, but they all have one similarity: There are many steps involved in providing a product or service.

Real estate companies provide a service rather than a product. They help people sell their homes. A real estate company's service includes advertising, finding prospective buyers, showing the home to interested parties, helping the seller and potential buyer agree on a selling price, and arranging to have legal documents drawn up to complete the sale. In addition, the company works with the seller to make sure the proper deeds and other papers are completed to change ownership of the property.

The homeowner pays for the services provided by a real estate company. If the services are not done correctly, a buyer may not be found for the house, or legal problems could develop after the home has been sold. Each person working in a real estate office needs to know how all the services are provided. Even the newest employee, whose job it is to type up information sheets about the houses the company is trying to sell, needs to understand the process involved in selling a home. By knowing the services provided, he or she has a better understanding of what information needs to be typed on the sheets and what can be left off. The employee will know if he or she has not been provided with all the information necessary to do the job correctly. Remember, it is the *YOUR* responsibility to learn about your company's products and services.

Working for a company means more than just doing a job. It means doing a job that helps the company produce services and products to meet the needs of its customers. By knowing *why* you are doing your job, you can do it better and help your company grow and prosper—which will allow you to grow and prosper too. You are preparing yourself to assume the responsibilities of other jobs in the company.

There are many steps involved in producing a product—learn ALL the steps.

Finding a Mentor and an Advocate

The amount of money a person receives for doing a job is usually related to how well they do their job. How well a person does their job has to do with how hard he or she tries and how much he or she knows about the work. If you could find a way to learn about your job more quickly, would it increase your chances to make more money? You bet it would! Employers pay for knowledge of the job. The more you know, the more valuable you are. Let's look at a way you can learn your job more quickly—and possibly make more money.

When a person goes starts a new job, he or she is expected to have some basic skills—the skills of a good worker. As time goes on, the worker learns more about the job and ways to do it better and faster. The employee who has been with the company for ten years knows much more about the job than the employee who has only been on the job ninety days.

If you are the new employee, there are only two ways for you to know as much about the job as the ten year veteran. The first way to learn all that information is to work at the job ten years. A lot of learning is done by trial and error; you try something and do it sort of right, but the next time you do it a little better. Maybe you do something exactly right the first time, but the next time you try something new, do it wrong and have to do it over. It is a slow process, but that is how most employees learn their job. How else can you learn all this information?

The second way to learn your job is to have a teacher—someone to teach you about your job. Another name for a teacher is a **mentor**. A mentor is a person who has a lot of experience and who shares his or her knowledge with you. Most companies have employees who can act as mentors. You should identify them and ask them for help. Who would make a good mentor? Remember the employee who had worked for the company for ten years? That person very likely may be a good mentor. How can you tell if someone has the qualities to be a good mentor?

Identifying a Mentor

To identify a mentor, you have to know the people with whom you work, and develop good working relationships with them. If you are working on developing a communication system, helping others, and learning about your company, you are well on your way to identifying a mentor. As you learn about your fellow workers and their job skills it will become obvious to you who could be a mentor. As long as a person has the knowledge, ability to teach, and a willingness to help you, he or she will probably be a good mentor. You will need to determine which people have these **attributes**.

It takes time to determine the extent of a fellow worker's knowledge. Therefore, you must be observant and a good listener. As time goes on, those who are knowledgeable and experienced will be the ones to whom others go for information. Listen to what the knowledgeable people are saying and use this information to determine if they understand the big picture. Are they aware of the relationship between the job they are describing and final product? You will soon learn which employees simply talk as if they know what they are doing, and which ones really know their jobs. Mentors usually stand out as the people others go to when they need help. There may be more than one mentor in your company—you can learn from all of them.

Determining a person's ability to teach also requires careful observation. Once you have determined which workers are knowledgeable about their jobs, you will want to observe how they answer questions. Ask yourself these questions about your potential mentor:

- Is the person a good listener? Does he or she take time to make sure they understand the question that has been asked?

- Does he or she explain the answer carefully? Does he or she take time to make sure the person asking the question understands what is being said?

- Is the person willing to repeat his or her answer in another way that is more easily understood?

- Does the person seem patient? Does he or she allow the listener to think about the explanation?

- If the person doesn't know the answer, will he or she admit it and be willing to try and find out the answer if it is something he or she should know?

If the person has the ability to listen and answer questions, he or she will probably be a good mentor.

Finally, a good mentor will be willing to help. Why would someone want to stop his own work to help you? Most people who take pride in their work enjoy sharing their knowledge with others. They have worked hard to gain their experience, and enjoy knowing that others are interested in them and what they know. They take pride in their work and want to see others do their job right. Good workers not only are concerned about their work, they are concerned about the company and its success. If other employees are doing poor work, it can affect both them and the company.

Begin your quest by identifying individuals who might make a good mentor. The first person to consider is your boss. However, if your boss is not someone who has the qualities of a mentor, don't rely on him or her for all your information. Look for other employees who have been with the company for awhile. Get to know them and help them if you can. If you are lucky, they will be willing to help you learn ten years' worth of knowledge in much less time.

Can you find a teacher to help you with your job?

Identifying an Advocate

A supervisor's job is to teach and guide his or her employees. Your supervisor's ultimate goal should be to help you become the best employee you can be. A good boss also will be your advocate. An **advocate** is someone who works for your success and who speaks on your behalf when decisions are being made that involve your future on the job. Advocates tell others about your positive attributes.

When individuals are under consideration for a promotion or pay increase, several people are usually involved in the final decision. In most companies, several managers will meet to discuss any changes that are to be made. They will discuss which employees should be involved in the change. For example, someone may need to be transferred to another department. This creates an open position that needs to be filled. If your boss is your advocate and feels you are qualified for the new position, he or she will tell others about you and the skills you possess to meet the needs of the new job. Your boss can talk about your work history and your attitude toward your work. He or she also can point out how quickly you learn and how willing you are to take on new challenges.

The opposite situation also may exist; the managers may discuss eliminating a position. They will talk about the different employees, deciding which ones should remain and which one they will have to let go. If your boss is familiar with your work, he or she can recommend that you remain with the company. This may be the most important time to have an advocate telling others about your strengths and work history.

What happens if your boss is not a good mentor or advocate? Is there anything you can do to improve your situation? Yes! You can find others to fill these roles. Successful employees find alternate mentors and advocates to help them learn their jobs or speak for them when important decisions are being made.

You may have several mentors. You may also have more than one advocate. Remember the supervisors you met when you were visiting other departments? They may make good advocates. An advocate is someone whose opinion is respected by others and who knows your skills and work history.

Identifying an advocate means determining who is respected by other managers and letting them know about the kind of work you do. Just as you will learn about the informal chain of command, you will learn which managers and employees have the respect of management. Sometimes a supervisor or manager does not do his or her job very well. Some managers don't know their employees very well and don't even know much about what their workers do. This weakness is usually recognized by the other managers. A poor supervisor is not going to be a very good advocate—especially if they don't have the respect of the other managers. If you have a supervisor who is not a good advocate, find someone else to speak for you.

Finding an alternate advocate involves the same skills as learning about the company, identifying a mentor, and building an information system; namely, observing, listening, and asking questions. After you have been with a company for a while, you will begin to identify individuals who will make good advocates. Once you know who they are, develop a plan to keep them informed about you and the quality of work you do for the company. When the time comes to advocate for you, they will know what to say and others will listen.

Everything that has been presented in this chapter is designed to help you succeed on the job. Each step in the process of learning about your company is only part of a puzzle that shows you how to work with those around you. Developing an information network will help you find an advocate or mentor, and helping others will improve your working relationship with management and co-workers. It's all part of the puzzle. Learn all the parts and put them together so you can be the kind of employee who is recommended for promotions, new challenges, and bigger paychecks.

*To see the big picture, you need
to know the parts of the puzzle.*

Study Questions

1. What are some of the ways you can learn how your company is organized?

2. What is the informal chain of command? How can you use it to your benefit?

3. Why is a weak link in the chain of command a problem for an employee? How can he or she get around that problem?

4. How can an employee develop a communication network? Why is this important?

5. What is the difference between a mentor and an advocate?

Chapter Seven:
Working for Your Boss

Chapter Objectives

In this chapter you will:

1. Learn the importance of knowing your boss' job and how to work successfully with him or her.

2. Learn how to make your boss' job easier.

3. See why working for a successful boss is working for a happy boss.

4. Learn the importance of finding ways to do your job better.

5. Find out how to deal with a lack of recognition for your good work and still be a good employee.

We look for people who are promotable. These are adaptable people who are willing to volunteer, pitching in beyond their job description.
                                    Deidre Abair
                                    Atlantic Journal and Constitution

Doing Your Job

"I am only doing my job." Have you ever heard someone say that? What does "doing your job" mean? To some people, it means going through the steps that are necessary to produce a product or service. To others, it means a great deal more.

To do your job well, you must understand everything involved with your job—not just the steps that *appear* to be your job. Only doing the minimum amount of work that is required to complete a task leads to **mediocrity**. Mediocrity does not lead to success; it leads to more mediocrity. Set your goals high and *LEARN HOW TO DO YOUR JOB WELL.*

Learning About Your Boss' Job

Your job includes working with others. Good employees know how to work well with those around them; they also know how to get along with their bosses.

Your employer or supervisor is a very important part of your job. He or she gives you assignments, evaluates your work, and recommends you for promotions and pay increases. The way in which you relate to your boss will have a major impact on your job success. A good relationship with your boss can make your job enjoyable and rewarding. If you like your work, but do not get along well with your boss, you will dread working with him or her. This will have a negative affect on your attitude about your work. Many people quit jobs they like because they don't get along with their employers.

For you to be successful, you must develop a good working relationship with your boss. Good **interpersonal skills**, or people skills, will help you a lot. One way to cultivate these skills is to imagine yourself in your boss' position. This may give you a better understanding of his or her actions.

Learning about your boss' job
will improve your working relationship.

In order to understand your boss, it is important to know what his or her job involves. A supervisor does more than tell people what to do; he or she must keep the operation moving smoothly. The supervisor coordinates all the operations within his or her area of responsibility. When your boss gives you an assignment, he or she is fitting your work into a plan that leads to an overall goal. For example, if it is your task to assemble a part that will be a portion of a finished product, your work must be done in time to add it to other parts. Your supervisor may tell you that your job is to complete four parts by ten o'clock. He or she knows how much time is available before your part is needed for the next phase of the operation. Your boss is not telling you this simply to order you around; there is a schedule to be met!

Imagine you are the supervisor of an automobile assembly line. Each day your crew of workers must assemble and build three automobiles. Your job is to make sure this task is completed each day. How would you do the job?

First you would determine the steps that are necessary to complete a car. What part goes on first? What part goes on last? If the steps are done incorrectly, the job may not be finished in time. If you put someone on a job that he or she can't handle, mistakes may slow down your production. As the supervisor, you must decide the order in which tasks are to be completed and who should do those tasks.

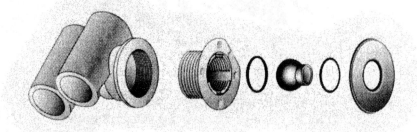

A boss' job is to make sure all the steps are completed in the right order and at the right time.

After you determine the order in which parts are to be attached to the frame of the car, you assign individuals to complete the various tasks: Ed is given axles and wheels; Ruth is in charge of springs; Heather is responsible for steering mechanisms; Mel and Linda install the engines; Chris and William handle the transmissions. Your entire crew is assigned a job. Each person has an assigned task that will lead to a completed car.

As work starts on the cars, you check on your crew to make sure things are being done properly. As time goes on, you may determine that Heather would work better with Linda on engines and Mel would be better on steering mechanisms, so you change their jobs. Some jobs are more critical than others; you give those to your most dependable workers.

You may have meetings with your workers and ask them to look for ways to improve the operation. When they make suggestions, it is your job to consider them and make adjustments if they are appropriate. These adjustments may involve changing the way jobs are done or moving people to different jobs. You may make adjustments because the engineers have redesigned a part and it must be attached differently or at a different step in the process. Your job is to keep the process moving smoothly by matching workers to jobs, and jobs to the entire process.

Other factors may affect your job as supervisor. As production schedules change, you must adjust your part of the operation to meet those changes. You may have to add more workers or extend their working hours. Or you may have to lay off some workers or cut their hours. If production costs are too high, you may have to lower costs by changing the way things are being done to improve efficiency. Of course, this is a simplified example of a supervisor's job; the job is usually much more complicated. But, the idea to remember is that a boss does more than "boss people around." There are reasons for the directions bosses give to their employees.

*Try to understand the reasons behind
the directions your boss gives you.*

As an employee, it is to your advantage to understand your
boss' job. If you understand what your boss is trying to do, it
will be easier for you to help them reach their goals. If they
reach their goal, you can reach one of your goals—to gain the
respect of your boss. Creating a good working relationship
with your employer or supervisor is part of your job.

Many employees never take the time to learn about their boss'
job. You already know that it is important to learn about the
company, but it is just as important to learn about your boss'
job. Observe the operation of your department. What are

your supervisor's responsibilities? Who works for him or her? How do their jobs relate to each other? How does your department's work relate to that of other departments? To whom does your boss report? As you answer these questions you will begin to understand more about your boss' job.

Helping Your Boss Succeed

If you understand your boss' job, it will be easier to find ways to help him or her succeed. The old saying, "Your success is my success," applies to working with your boss. By helping your boss succeed, you will ultimately benefit too. Most successful employees will tell you that a successful boss is usually a happy boss; and an unsuccessful boss is usually an unhappy one. Which one would you like as *your* supervisor?

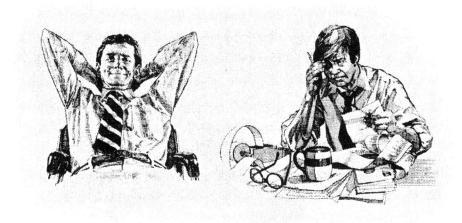

For which boss would you rather work?

In previous chapters, you learned a number of ways to be successful on the job. Some of those relate to helping your boss be successful. If you do your job right, you will be helping your boss do his or her job right. As we review ways to help your boss, you will see some ideas that have already been presented as well as some new ones. The important thing to remember is that when your boss asks you or someone else to do things, his or her directions are part of an overall plan. You are part of that plan and can make it work by doing your job right.

One way to help your supervisor is to learn to be less dependent upon him or her. As you learn how to do your job, you should be able to make more decisions on your own—without requiring your boss' time. To learn your job more quickly, be sure you understand the directions that are given to you. Repeat the directions to assure that you and your boss are communicating with each other. Ask questions if you are not sure what to do. You are less likely to make mistakes when you clearly understand your assignment, and your boss will appreciate not having to spend a lot of time to help you fix your mistakes.

As you become more confident in your knowledge of your job, you can rely even less on your boss for direction. Don't be afraid to take on new tasks if you are sure you understand what needs to be done. Don't wait to be asked—volunteer to assist with other tasks. Once you have developed a good working relationship with your boss, it will be much easier for you to see what needs to be done. If your boss has confidence in your abilities, he or she will appreciate your **initiative** and sense of responsibility. Supervisors often complain about employees who see something that needs to be done but wait for someone else to tell them to do it.

*I sure get tired of telling my employees what
to do. Can't they see what needs to be done?*

Supervisors and managers appreciate employees who are not
afraid to make decisions. There will be many opportunities for
you to evaluate a situation and then make a decision. For
example, you may be assigned a task that requires help from
someone. If you know your job and how it relates to others,
you can decide to ask someone else to help you with your
assignment. Your boss may not be available to ask who
should help you. Your choice is to ask for help or do nothing
until your boss returns. If you have a good working relationship with your boss and understand what he or she is trying

to accomplish, you could confidently make the decision to ask for help. The person helping you will more than likely be the same person your boss would ask if he or she were available. By making a decision to ask for help, you **demonstrate** leadership skills and don't waste time waiting for your boss to return.

What if it turns out your boss would have asked someone else to help you? What should you do? The best thing to do would be to explain to your boss why you picked the person you did. Then you could ask why he or she would pick someone else. This way you demonstrate to your boss that you want to learn from your mistakes so you can make the right choice next time. A good manager will appreciate your questions as well as your desire to improve your decision-making skills. Taking the initiative and making decisions is a trait most employers respect. It also can lead to promotions.

Finding Ways to Make Your Boss' Job Easier

To help your boss succeed, you should look for ways to make his or her job easier. Why should you try to make things easier for your boss? Remember—*your boss' success is your success.* Your desire to help your supervisor should be rooted in a sincere desire to help your employer; but let's be honest, you may end up working for someone who is a poor manager. Should you still help that person? Yes! Helping your boss can do nothing but help you too.

Volunteer to help in tasks for which you are qualified—even if they are not in an area directly related to your job. By volunteering, you will accomplish several things. The most important thing you will accomplish is that you will give your boss more time to do his or her job properly. This can be especially important when **deadlines** have to be met. Good bosses usually **appreciate** any help they can get as it allows

them to take care of other tasks. Most supervisors have a
lot of responsibilities that require a great deal of their time.
Helping them will take some of the job pressure off of them.
In addition to giving your boss the opportunity to become a
better manager, you will be gaining his or her appreciation.

Supervisors have a lot of responsibilities.
Find ways to help your boss.

By assisting your boss, you demonstrate that you are willing
to help. Your boss will remember you as a dependable
employee. Some employees have a reputation for not being
helpful. In fact, supervisors soon learn who can be relied
upon for help and who should be avoided. By volunteering to
help, you will be seen as one of the reliable people. You will
probably end up doing more work than the person who is not
willing to help, but as time goes on you will have a better
working relationship with your boss. This will increase the
amount of satisfaction you receive from your job. Please note,

however, that it is important to be sincere in your desire to help. Most people can see through someone who is volunteering simply for self-serving gain. If your boss perceives that you are merely using the situation to make points with him or her, your motives and honesty may be questioned.

Volunteering to help your boss gives you the opportunity to learn more about your job and other jobs in your department or company. As you do more for your boss, your level of job knowledge will increase. The more you know about the work around you, the more valuable you become to your supervisor and the company. You will soon discover that your reputation for being willing to do tasks that are not a part of your job will be a valuable asset to you. The news will get around that you can be relied upon to do the best you can, no matter what you are assigned to do. With this kind of reputation, your boss and others will be happy to advocate for you. But remember, the main reason for helping your boss is to make his or her job easier.

What are some ways you can make your boss' job easier? Many supervisors have a variety of responsibilities. These responsibilities may include such tasks as simple record keeping or filing. These are duties for which you could easily volunteer. If you work in a retail store, taking inventory or reconciling the cash register are jobs you might volunteer to do. Many employees in retail stores have expanded their jobs or moved on to better jobs by volunteering to do simple record-keeping tasks.

Perhaps your company receives many catalogs or lists of parts and materials. You could organize these materials into some kind of system that allows quick and easy access to the information contained in these documents. Managers often are so busy they give organizing such materials a low priority and catalogs pile up in a very disorganized manner. When your boss does need to find information in the documents, it may take a long time to find what is needed. Make his or her job easier—volunteer to organize the materials. It might require more work, but in the long run it may make life a little easier for both of you.

No matter what type of company you work for, there will be many opportunities to help your boss. You may not receive any immediate rewards for your efforts, but you can feel satisfied in knowing you helped make another person's job a little easier. Remember, doing your job means working with others. Making your boss' job easier *is* part of your job, so do the best you can.

Knowing Your Boss

Everyone has opinions. They have opinions about politics, religion, education, taxes, marriage, children, work, etc. Your supervisor is no different than anyone else. His or her opinion about most things may or may not be important to you. However, there are certain opinions which *should* concern you. Your boss' opinions about the company, his or her job, and the employees are *very* important. One of your tasks is to learn how your boss feels about his or her job, the company, and anything else that relates to your job. Does your boss feel strongly about employees who complain all the time? Does he or she like workers who are organized? Does he or she favor employees who come in a little early to prepare for the day's activities? It is your responsibility to find out how your boss feels about work related issues. Here is an example of an employee who failed to do this.

Cara worked for a company for six months. Her boss was a nice enough person, asking little more than the minimum from Cara. Cara worked from eight o'clock in the morning to five o'clock in the afternoon. If she didn't finish a task by five o'clock she would set it aside until the next day—even if it would only take another five minutes to complete it. Sometimes Cara's boss needed something finished that day, but Cara always left at 5:00 whether or not the task was completed. Her boss was somewhat disappointed, but didn't say anything.

A new position opened up in Cara's department and she applied for the job. Another employee, John, applied for it also. John had been with the company about the same length of time as Cara. When the notice of the new job was removed from the bulletin board, Cara asked her boss who had been assigned to the new job. She was dismayed to hear that John had been chosen. She could not understand why John got the job instead of her. In frustration, she asked her boss why she hadn't been recommended for the job. Her boss informed her that the job required working more than eight hours on some occasions and she didn't feel Cara was interested in the extra time required for that type of job.

Later that day, Cara saw John and congratulated him on his promotion. John thanked her and said he was looking forward to the challenge of the new job. He then said, "I guess putting in extra time on those projects paid off!" Cara asked him what projects he was talking about. John said, "You know our boss, she hates to have things unfinished when they can be done with a few minutes extra work. Sometimes I stayed an extra few minutes after quitting time to finish certain projects. She told me that before she became a supervisor, she would always try to finish a project before she left work. When I heard that, I knew it would be to my benefit to put in a few extra minutes and get the job finished instead of waiting until the next day."

Cara could argue that she is only required to work until five o'clock, and she would be right. However, what she failed to consider was her boss' strong feelings about not putting something off until the next day if it could be finished with a few more minutes of effort. Cara didn't pay attention to her boss' opinion. Bosses are human and may have strong opinions about what they expect from their employees. If these opinions are not unreasonable, it is up to you to learn about them and adjust the way you do things.

Learning to Improve Your Work

Most companies look for ways to improve their operations. Perhaps the order in which tasks are done may be changed to accomplish more in less time. Producing a product or service in less time usually means more profit to the company. If a business generates more profit, the employers are more likely to increase employee wages or expand their business. This creates additional opportunities for employees to work at better and higher paying jobs. You can help your company be more efficient and profitable.

As you get more experienced at your job, you should look for ways to do it better. Many workers have the attitude that it isn't their responsibility to improve their work. They argue that their job only is to do what they are told to do. *They are wrong!* Each worker's job includes finding ways to improve. It may not say that in the job description, but it *IS* part of the job. If every employee finds ways to improve his or her work, the company will stay competitive and be more likely to remain in business. If every employee just does what he or she is told and never looks for better ways to get the work done, the company will be less likely to stay competitive. Let's see how this attitude of doing your best affects a business operation.

In the previous example of building cars, you were the supervisor. You had the responsibility to make sure that your crew built three cars per day. Imagine that Mary, a supervisor in another car company, also must build three cars per day to compete with your company. Each of you would work very hard to make sure your crews meet the company goals of three cars per day. Now consider what would happen if Mary's employees looked for ways to do their jobs better.

Lets say that each of Mary's employees finds one or two ways to complete their assignments more quickly. If she listens to these ideas and combines all of the suggested improvements, it might save one half hour per day. Every sixteen days, Mary's crew will save a total of eight hours, or one eight hour work day. That means that an additional three cars could be built every sixteen days!

*Making suggestions about ways to do your
job better is good for you and your company.*

In any business, if you can build more product than before without increasing your costs, you are producing each product at a lower cost. If you can produce at a lower cost, you can sell your product for less money or make more product. Now Mary's company is able to sell cars for less money than your company. By selling cars at a lower price, they attract more customers. More customers means more profit. Mary's company is making more profit and continues to attract more customers. Because of the company's success they are able to increase production, pay overtime, and create new jobs.

In the meantime, *your* crew's attitude is that they only do what they are told. They don't look for ways to do their jobs better. If you can't find a way to build cars at the same price as the competition (Mary's company), your employer will have to cut back on costs by laying off workers and eliminating your shift. Your job is to improve production and lower its costs. Certainly you could look at your employees' jobs and suggest ways to make them more efficient, but your employees might have more **insight** regarding their jobs than you do. Furthermore, if your crew is not interested in improvement, they may resist any changes you suggest. Which set of employees would you rather have working for you?

This may seem like an extreme example, but businesses face this type of competition every day. They look for employees who will help them stay ahead of the competition. Here are some ways you can do your job better:

1. **Look for ways to be more efficient in what you are doing.** Are there some steps in your job that could be changed to save time?

2. **Learn the entire operation, and look for ways to make that process more efficient.** Are there steps in the process that could be improved? Maybe your step could come before or after another step in the process.

3. **Talk to your co-workers and discuss ways to improve the process.** You may not think of an idea by yourself, but a new idea may appear with input from others.

4. **If your job requires specific skills that can be learned elsewhere, look for ways to broaden your knowledge.** Read articles in books and magazines or take classes that will increase your job skills.

5. **Don't be afraid to discuss your job responsibilities with your boss.** If you don't understand why you are required to perform a certain step, find out why that step is important. You can't find ways to improve your job if you don't know why you are doing specific aspects of it. Be careful that you don't look as if you are complaining about your job when you talk to your boss. Let him or her know you are asking questions so you can better understand your job.

6. **If possible, learn about the cost of producing the products and services in your company.** Keep the cost of doing business in mind as you work. Knowing the cost of an operation will make you more aware of ways to improve your efficiency.

7. **Challenge yourself to do better.** Look at your work as if it can be improved through your efforts. Don't settle for doing things as usual.

Attract Attention by Doing More Than is Expected

By making an effort to improve your work, you set an example for those who work with you. It may be that your supervisor doesn't realize the importance of encouraging workers to find better ways to do their jobs. Your interest in doing your job better will catch on with other workers and your boss. Furthermore, you will be recognized as a good employee. Fellow workers may have more respect for your work, and your boss may give you the opportunity to take on more complex jobs. Recognition from your boss usually leads to a higher income.

There may be times when your efforts to do your best at your job may *not* be recognized immediately. Some bosses have not learned the importance of acknowledging employees' efforts on a regular basis. They may not say anything to you until it is time to review your progress with the company. This process takes place once a year, and is called an annual review. However, in some companies a semi-annual review occurs every six months. Furthermore, if you are a new employee, your boss may review your progress after only ninety days. Whichever process your company uses, don't be surprised if your boss waits until the review to acknowledge your job efforts.

It is unfortunate that some supervisors don't recognize an employee's efforts on a regular basis. If you find yourself in this situation, you need to find ways to reward yourself for the extra efforts you have made. One way of doing this is to set goals and congratulate yourself when you reach your goal. This way you can acknowledge your efforts and feel a sense of accomplishment.

Finding ways to do your job better
is one of the roads to success on the job.

Telling friends and family is another way of receiving recognition for your extra effort. Telling someone who is interested in you about your experiences at work is not bragging. If your boss is giving you more responsibility at work, share that information with a friend. When you find a better way to do your job, share that success with your family. Eventually you will probably be recognized for your efforts. The important thing is that you have a feeling of accomplishment at work.

Knowing your job and doing it well will give you a feeling of success. Helping those you work with will help you feel like a part of the organization. You will need to apply your interpersonal skills to a variety of situations in the jobs of today and tomorrow. These skills will help you excel at your job. Learn about your job and do your best. Help your boss and others do their jobs better. The result will be your success, their success, and a sense of accomplishment. Try it, it works.

Study Questions

1. Why is it important to know about your boss' job?

2. What is wrong with the statement, "My boss just likes to give directions."

3. If you help your boss succeed, how will this help you?

4. How can you learn about your boss' likes and dislikes? Why is this important?

5. What are some ways an employee can help a company become more competitive?

Chapter Eight:

Dealing With Job Challenges

Chapter Objectives

In this chapter you will:

1. Become aware of the challenges of working with others.

2. See how learning from others will benefit you on the job.

3. Find ways to avoid gossip in the workplace.

4. Learn how to deal with criticism and praise.

5. Find out how to cope with anger, frustration, and boredom.

6. Learn how to respond to prejudice and discrimination.

7. Find ways to deal with job change.

*We are working with a quality team concept—working
in a team environment for solving work problems and
interpersonal problems.*

Michael Badka
Motorola Corporation

Anyone who takes his or her job seriously will tell you
that working with other people can be a challenge. You can
avoid people in your personal life if you wish; but on the job,
especially in today's world of work, you can't avoid working
with people. Some people you work with will be friendly and
accommodating, while others may not be helpful at all. Part
of your job is to learn how to deal with your fellow workers
successfully. To do this, you will need to develop ways of
dealing with different situations and individual personalities.

Developing good **peer** relationships is the key to meeting the
challenges of your job. If you work well with those around
you, you will be better equipped to deal with the variety of
situations you encounter on the job. If you do not learn how
to work with others, you will be less effective in your work and
you will probably not be very happy. Good employees look for
ways to meet the challenges of their job.

Making Friends as a New Employee

When you start a new job, you may feel uncomfortable
because you don't know any of your co-workers and your
surroundings are unfamiliar. It is like going into a new part
of town or a new city. The first day on the job you will be
meeting new people and trying to learn a great deal of

information in a short period of time. Some of the people you meet that first day will be friendly, while others may not. As the days go on, you will begin to work with some of the people you met in your first days on the job. Other workers may talk to you in the lunch room or when they pass you in the halls. Some of these people will help you learn about the company and your job. This is a learning and growing time for a new employee—a time when you probably will want to make friends quickly.

As you meet new people, you will consciously or subconsciously begin to determine who you want to make friends with and who you don't think would be a friend. It is perfectly natural to want to make friends. Good friends make us feel comfortable and give us a sense of security.

If one employee happens to show you more attention than others, it will be easy to develop a friendship with that person. This new friend may know a lot about the company, and his or her information will make you feel more comfortable in your new job. However, as you begin to spend more and more time with your new friend, a situation may develop that you do not want to happen.

Spending all or most of your time with one employee may make other employees feel that you are not friendly and that you don't like them. Even those who offered you little help when you first came to work may wonder why you spend so much time with only one person. You may not even realize this situation has developed. You are not playing favorites, you are just getting to know someone who has been helpful and made you feel comfortable in your new job. How can you avoid offending others in this way?

Meeting New People

As you meet new people, learn their names and show a sincere interest in them. Take every opportunity to meet as many people as possible. Make a habit of joining different people at lunch if you feel welcome. Sit in different places in the lunch room or go to lunch with different people when you have the opportunity. Increase your chances of meeting others by visiting different parts of the company, store, or building in which you work. Be friendly! Introduce yourself to others, and tell them you are new and want to learn what they do for the company. This way you will not limit yourself to only knowing one or two fellow employees. People who are truly interested in being your friend will still be helpful to you even if you continue to meet others. And, as time goes on, you will develop closer relationships with workers who have some of the same interests you have.

Meet as many new people as you can.

Meeting new people will allow you to develop friendships that are based on your **compatibility** with those people instead of simply latching on to the first person who shows some interest. Be careful! Don't try to push people into friendships with you— you will only succeed in making people avoid you. Time is the key element here. Give friendship time to develop while getting to know the other people with whom you work.

Look for Honesty and Sincerity in Others

Making friends at work is an interesting process. People you work with can help you in various ways. Some may volunteer to help you learn about your job and the company, and others will help you if you ask them. Which workers should you trust, and which workers may have other reasons for helping you? It takes some time to answer this question. You must consider all your fellow workers to be people you can trust until you find proof to the contrary. Most people are fair and honest, but there may be some people who only *appear* to want to help you. As you meet new people, you will discover who is sincere and honest. These are people with whom you will develop long-term relationships. They will make your job interesting and enjoyable. Fellow workers who sincerely want to help you, and who expect nothing in return, can be a real asset on the job. They will help you and you will help them. This is what good working relationships are all about. Look for honest, sincere workers who will help you fit into your new job.

Watch Out for the Rumor Mill

Gossiping about others is a favorite pastime of some workers. They enjoy talking about what is wrong with other people; they feed on each other, adding to the negative comments others have said. This is dangerous territory. It can be very tempting to get involved with the **rumor mill** because others seem interested in what you have to say. Unfortunately these people may only show an interest because they think you might give them some juicy information to pass on to others. People in rumor mills are not interested in the truth, they only want to hear the latest gossip. Workers who gossip about others do it because they feel important when they have information others want to hear.

One of the worst things you can do is to talk in a negative way about other employees. By passing on negative information you stand a very good chance of hurting someone else. Furthermore, you may find that the information isn't even true. If your employer learns you are making negative comments about the company, he or she is not likely to give you opportunities to grow and advance with the business. Your negative comments may come back to haunt you.

Talking in a negative way about others may not only hurt them, it may **jeopardize** your chances of developing a good working relationship with them. If someone you have gossiped about hears what you have been saying, he or she may be very reluctant to cooperate with you. Even if you are sure the rumor you heard about someone is true, don't get caught up in the game of saying negative things about others. If you join a group of workers and discover their only interest is in talking about what is wrong with the company or other workers, find a different group. Associating with negative people will only lead you to be more negative. If you feel you must talk to someone about things at work, take your discussion home where it won't be passed on to others.

Gossip can hurt both you and others.

Coping With Criticism

We all have to deal with criticism at various times. A family member may accuse us of doing or not doing something; someone in school may criticize something we did; or a boss may not be happy with our performance. Depending on the situation, we react to criticism in different ways. Receiving criticism at work can be very disturbing. After all, we do our best at work so we can keep our job and earn an income. If it appears our job is threatened by a boss' criticism, we may react in a way that does not benefit us. Therefore, it becomes important to learn how to deal with criticism in positive and productive ways.

Learning how to cope with criticism is important.

Emotions can affect the way we hear what someone is saying when they criticize us. Emotions can make us see criticism as a personal attack rather than a complaint about something we did. For example, if your boss tells you not to take on any new assignments because you can't get them done, you may believe he or she is unhappy with your work.

Wouldn't you find it upsetting if your boss said that to you? The problem is, your boss may think you do good work, but tend to take on more than you can complete. You simply are doing too much. That's certainly different from not doing good work. How can one statement have two or more meanings? Your interpretation of your boss' comments may be influenced by emotional reaction. Someone was challenging your work. You know you do good work, yet you immediately believed someone thought the quality of your work was poor. Your emotions didn't let you review the other possibilities of what your boss meant when she criticized you. Therefore, instead of asking questions, you either remain silent or argue with the person criticizing you.

Emotion is a very powerful factor when receiving criticism. How can we minimize the effects of our emotions when an employer or co-worker seems to be criticizing us? The secret to receiving criticism is to relax and lower your emotional level. As the person is talking to you, look them in the eye and *listen* to what they are saying. Relax your body, face the person squarely, and don't cross your arms. People who feel threatened tend to look away and cross their arms in defense.

As the person is talking to you, process what he or she is saying. Try not to let your personal feelings get involved. If you don't understand the criticism, ask questions to clarify what is being said. Be careful not to challenge the person— just clarify his or her meaning. You will have a chance to challenge the statement after you have had time to process what has been said. The most important part of good communication is that it goes in both directions. You are receiving information to which you must respond. Try looking at the situation from the speaker's point of view, especially if it is your boss who is speaking. The speaker may have a unique perspective that has not occurred to you. If the person is right, acknowledge it and discuss the problem.

Don't apologize unnecessarily when admitting you have made a mistake. By apologizing over and over, you annoy the person talking and you may not be believable. It is best simply to say, "I am sorry." After apologizing, discuss what you will do differently in the future. Make suggestions on ways to improve your performance and ask the person if those ideas would resolve the problem. This way the discussion will center on the problem and not you. Remember, *YOU as a person are OK*; it was your performance that was questioned.

*Explain the facts if your critic has
the wrong information. Don't argue.*

If the criticism is incorrect, clarify the situation in a calm and
friendly voice so the person can better understand all the facts
in the situation. Many times, criticism is simply a result of a
misunderstanding. Clarifying the facts usually solves this
problem. Sometimes an incorrect criticism is the result of
another person's problem. He or she may be upset about
another situation and take their anger out on you. The only
way to deal with this situation is to restate the sender's main
points of the criticism, and then deal with each one in a rational
manner—without emotion. Save your emotions for later.

If the situation is such that you cannot deal with it without
expressing a lot of emotion, acknowledge that you have heard
what has been said. If it is appropriate, tell the person you
want to think about what he or she has said, and you would
like to discuss it later. After you have had time to calm down
and think through your discussion with the other person, jot
down your thoughts about the conversation.

With these ideas in front of you, you can do one of two things. First, you can plan your response to their criticism and share it with them at the next opportunity. Second, you can prepare a written response to their criticism. Put your written response away for some time and then reread it when your mind is fresh and not filled with the emotional thoughts you had when you were writing. Reading your thoughts later will help you realize how emotion influenced your thinking. You may want to rewrite your response before giving it to your critic. Like so many things we do when dealing with others, it is better to think things through and have a plan. Here are the steps involved in dealing with criticism:

- Relax and maintain your emotions.

- Face the person who is talking to you. Don't cross your arms.

- Look the speaker in the eye and listen carefully.

- Try to see the speaker's point of view.

- Repeat the main points the speaker made to be sure everyone is in agreement about what was said.

- Decide if you are receiving criticism or a verbal attack.

- Accept responsibility to change if it is warranted.

- If it is only a verbal attack, **refute** the points made by the critic in a calm voice, or ask to respond later after you have written down your response.

If you receive a written criticism, you can use the same techniques—just modify them to the situation. Good communication requires that you respond to criticism. The worst thing you can do is store up your anger. You may unintentionally release your anger by criticizing a fellow worker or member of your family.

Responding to Praise

Receiving praise is certainly more enjoyable than receiving criticism. However, reacting in the wrong way to praise can have negative consequences as well. If someone compliments you on work you have done, thank them and acknowledge that you enjoy your work. In this way you let them know you appreciate their interest. You also show them that you believe good work is part of the job.

When someone praises you, don't get carried away and go on and on about all the time you put in and the time you took away from your family—that only makes people uncomfortable. If you are doing good work and people acknowledge it, that is all that is necessary. People who talk about their great accomplishments annoy fellow employees and supervisors. Your work habits will demonstrate the quality of your work. If you have developed a good system of letting others know what you are doing, there is no need to brag about your accomplishments.

Don't over do the thank yous.

If your boss compliments you on a special effort you have made, you could say something like, "Thank you, I felt it was important to finish the project by Friday." In doing this, you are thanking your boss for the praise, and at the same time you are letting him or her know you made an effort beyond your usual quality work. Whether accepting criticism or praise, be sincere and modest in the way you react to the person communicating their message to you.

Dealing With Anger and Frustration

What do you think of when you hear the word conflict? A disagreement between people? When we disagree with someone on an issue, the result usually is conflict. Remember the *Korean conflict?* It was a war that resulted over a disagreement between two countries. When we have a disagreement with another person, we have a war on a much smaller scale. Wars in the workplace are not productive; they create anger and frustration—two emotions that can become real problems for people who work together eight hours a day.

Working with someone else requires agreement on how things should be done. If someone wants to do something differently than you do, you may become frustrated with them because you think your way is best. If he or she continues to resist your approach to dealing with the situation, you may become angry. It is here that the war begins. He or she wants to go in one direction to achieve a goal, and you want to go in another direction; or you may have a completely different goal in mind. You become frustrated when he or she fails to see what you are trying to accomplish, and he or she feels the same way about you. This is conflict—WAR! Your war may consist of verbal attacks, or it may be one of complete silence. In either case, you are not working together. In some cases you may get tired of the struggle and give in to the other person. If this happens, it may create a new level of aggression, and your ability to work with that other person may be reduced or lost. If you are working with your boss and you experience this kind of conflict, you could be in real trouble—he or she might decide that you are not the best person for that job. On the other hand, if the problem is with a co-worker, your abilities to complete your work successfully are limited. How can you avoid this kind of situation?

Dealing with the conflict is the only way to overcome anger and frustration. As long as conflict exists, there will be confusion, frustration, and anger. Learn to identify the conflicts that cause your anger.

Conflict leads to aggression.

How can you deal with conflict? If you are angry with someone, it may not be easy to resolve the situation. Strong emotions can prevent you from dealing with the situation in a rational manner; however, an unemotional approach is vital to solving any type of conflict. In fact, by discussing the problem with the other person, you may even find that one of you did not fully understand the situation. What you thought was a conflict may turn out to only be a misunderstanding! Here are some ways to be sure you understand the entire problem and agree on a solution.

1. With the other person, identify what needs to be accomplished.

2. Individually, identify your solutions to the situation or problem.

3. Compare your solutions with the other person and look for common elements.

4. Together, agree on areas in which you can modify your positions to reach a compromise.

By using a **systematic** approach to conflict, you usually can clarify the issues and come to an agreement.

When you are angry and cannot seem to work the problem out with the other person, there may be an **internal conflict**. Internal conflict is conflict within yourself. It can result from your interaction with another person, or it may be caused by **indecision**. For example, your boss may ask you to work overtime on Saturday. Later in the day a friend invites you to go skiing on Saturday. You need to work on Saturday because you need the money, yet you haven't been able to go skiing all winter and are really anxious to go. What do you do? If you cannot decide, you experience internal conflict.

Part of you thinks you should work, but another part of you thinks about how much fun you would have on the slopes. If your boss stops by and says, "I am trying to finish the work schedule for the rest of the week, and I need to know if you are going to work Saturday," you may get angry with him or her because you can't decide what to do. You are frustrated with yourself. In a state of frustration or anger, you may respond to your boss in an irritated tone. You aren't angry with your boss, but your tone certainly leaves the message that you are not happy with your boss talking to you at that particular moment.

Resolving a disagreement with yourself is much the same as coming to an agreement with someone else who does not agree with you. You need to work out your disagreements. Think about the conflict you are dealing with and find a solution.

If you have some bills that are due to be paid and don't have the money to pay them, or if you are simply trying to get ahead on your job, then working Saturday may be your only choice. Review the facts and make a decision, eliminating the conflict within yourself. The key to dealing with conflict is to determine what is causing the conflict and find a solution.

Remember, people often get angry when they feel they are not in control. Don't let the actions of others or unusual circumstances make you feel out of control. Stay calm and determine the best way to deal with the situation—remain in control of yourself.

Avoiding Boredom

New jobs usually interesting because we are learning new things. New jobs challenge us. As we become better at our jobs they provide a sense of accomplishment. At the end of the day, we can look our efforts and realize that we have contributed to the company. As time goes on, however, our work becomes routine. We may not be learning new things; and our accomplishments, though just as good, may not seem as important as when we first started. When this happens, we are feeling the effects of boredom. Boredom on the job is very dangerous. Workers who have become bored with their jobs often are careless and make mistakes. If your job becomes uninteresting the same things could happen to you. You may not realize that you are getting bored with your job until it is too late. When is it too late? It's too late when your boss talks to you about the low quality of your work, or worse—when you get fired.

Watch out for the signs of boredom.

This sounds bad doesn't it? It *can* be unless you learn to keep your job interesting. How do you keep your job interesting? One of the best ways is to keep learning. As long as your mind is being challenged by new ideas, you will stay interested in what you are doing. Some people will argue that once you have learned a job, there is nothing else to learn—*WRONG!* Once you have learned how to do your job, look for other activities you can do. Volunteer to do other jobs and learn them well. Learn more about the people around you, the jobs they do, and how their jobs relate to yours.

There is always something new to learn if you look for it. Challenge yourself in this area. What else can you learn? Can you improve the quality of the work you are doing? Is there a better way to do your job? You must always be looking for better ways to do your job. This keeps your work interesting.

If you have learned your job well and learned about others and their jobs, then maybe it is time to look for other jobs to do within the company. Apply for positions in other departments that interest you as they become available. If you have learned your job well and do excellent work, you should be a good candidate for a promotion.

Beware of the signs of boredom. If you don't look forward to going to work, you may no longer be challenged by your job. If you don't care about the quality of your work or have trouble concentrating on your job, you may need some new challenges. Don't get caught in the trap of job boredom. Keep yourself *challenged* by constantly learning and improving yourself.

Responding to Prejudice and Discrimination

A worker's attitude toward another has always been an area where conflicts can develop. If a worker seems to be working harder than necessary, another worker may feel threatened. If a boss asks an employee to join him or her for lunch, another worker may become jealous. If a newer employee is given a promotion before another employee with more seniority, the senior worker may blame the advancement on something other than the new employee's quality of work. People often try to find other reasons for another person's advancement, such as a person's **gender**, ethnic background, physical appearance, or any other factor they perceive as giving the employee an advantage. If they can attribute someone else's success to something other than hard work, they don't have to face their own failures.

Granted, sometimes favoritism *is* the reason a person is promoted. However, most of the time, promotions are given in recognition for quality of work and preparation for the job. Some workers come to the workplace with attitudes about others that are based on misinformation, rather than facts. For instance, some men believe they should receive more pay than women or receive an automatic advancement because they are "the head of the household." Sometimes people of one race feel they are better than others, and believe that they should be given privileges in the workplace. Likewise, older workers may feel that they should have advantages over younger workers who are not as competent as they are, while younger workers may believe the advantages should belong to them because older workers are stuck in their old ways of doing things. In each of these examples, people are using biased opinions to make a case for giving themselves advantages in the workplace.

Discriminatory attitudes are not new. Whenever people work closely together, these kinds of conflicts can develop. To help control this problem, several laws have been enacted to help those that are being treated unfairly on the job. The most far-reaching of these laws is the Title VII, Civil Rights Act of 1964, which prohibits discrimination on the basis of color, race, religion, sex, or national origin. This act affects decisions concerning hiring, placement, training, promotion, termination, and layoffs. The act also established the Equal Employment Opportunity Commission (EEOC) to enforce the law.

Other legislation that helps workers includes, the Equal Pay Act of 1963, which outlines a system for equal pay for men and women doing the same type of work; the Age Discrimination Act of 1967, which sets limits on discriminating against older workers; the Rehabilitation Act of 1973, which affects people with disabilities; and the 1980 Sexual Harassment Guidelines (added to the Civil Rights Act, Title VII), which outline employers' responsibilities regarding claims of sexual harassment.

Will these laws solve all the problems of prejudice on the job? Of course not. Some workers have spent a long time developing their negative attitudes about others. Laws, alone, are not going to cause people to change their minds. So what can you do if another worker or supervisor is treating you in a prejudicial way? The first thing to do is to work on the situation on a one-to-one basis. Some people have prejudices and don't even know it! They may not even think about their actions. For example, a co-worker may make a statement which implies that men should be paid more than women, regardless of their attitude and the quality of their work. If this happens, it may be effective to ask them questions about why they feel the way they do. For example, you might ask him if "head of household" is the proper **criteria** for a promotion or a raise. If so, does that mean that the worker with the most responsibilities at home should get the raise first? If both a man with a young family and an older man whose children have grown up are eligible for the same promotion, does he believe the young man should get the raise? With this line of questioning, you should be able to make the point that decisions that are based on anything other than attitude and quality of work are unfair.

Sexual harassment in the workplace is a problem that has gained more public attention in recent years. It is important for both sexes to realize that some actions are inappropriate in the work environment. Although one worker may think it is okay to tell jokes of a sexual nature, other workers may find this just as offensive as racial jokes. Subtle comments about a sexy outfit are offensive to many women. Constantly asking someone for a date could be considered sexual harassment. If any of these types of behavior become a problem for you, try to discuss the situation with the person causing your discomfort. If you explain in a calm and relaxed manner how such actions make you feel, you may be able to help the person understand his or her unconscious prejudices.

Sometimes it is necessary to challenge prejudice. If you know another person has made negative remarks, jokes, etc., about you, it may be appropriate for you to talk to them about what they are saying. If you are a good employee and have the respect of other workers, discussing negative comments with the person making them could cause him or her to think seriously about their attitude toward you. Doing nothing only allows the situation to continue.

If dealing with the problem directly does not work, you will have to go to your boss, mentor, or advocate and discuss the problem with him or her. These are people who may have some influence over the situation. Many companies have an **affirmative action** officer who is responsible for assuring that the company meets affirmative action laws. If your company has an affirmative action officer, he or she may be able to help you with your problem.

If you are unable to resolve your problem through these methods, you can fall back on the laws that protect workers from discriminatory practices. If you find yourself in this situation, you should obtain legal advice to determine how to use the law to deal with your problem.

Dealing With Challenges on the Job

From time to time our jobs may require us to learn a new job or move to a different location in the company. If this situation should occur on your job, there are two ways you can deal with the situation: The first is to get upset; the second is to see your new assignment as a challenge. Your decision on will determine how well you do your new job.

Many workers get upset when their company transfers them to another job or location. They fight the situation by complaining to others or doing poor work. It is unfortunate that people react to changes in this way because it doesn't allow them to grow. Instead of increasing their knowledge, they become bitter and less successful on the job.

How to Deal
With Job Challenges

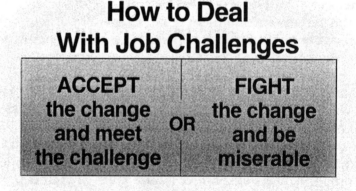

| ACCEPT the change and meet the challenge | OR | FIGHT the change and be miserable |

The choice is yours!

By accepting the job change as a challenge, you can learn more and grow as an individual. In most cases, a new job creates opportunities to learn new skills and work with different people. By maintaining a positive attitude, a transferred worker demonstrates to an employer that he or she is flexible and willing to take on new responsibilities and meet new challenges. Today's employers want workers who are willing to learn different jobs. If you are transferred by your company to another location or job, accept the challenge and do your best. When it comes time to promote an employee, you can be sure the complainer who would not accept a change won't be the one who is promoted. Employees who learn to accept job changes as challenges will be chosen over complainers every time.

As you learn more about your new job and begin to meet new people, it will become apparent that being a good employee means being a good *people person* who can deal with the challenges of the job. As our world becomes more complex and our jobs require us to make more adjustments, those who fight the change and get frustrated with problems will not be happy with their jobs. Learn to meet the challenges of your job and enjoy your work. If you have a full-time job, you can expect to work at least eight hours a day. That's about one-third of your life! You can spend a third of your life unhappy, or you can spend that time learning and growing.

Study Questions

1. When starting a new job, what is wrong with avoiding others once you have made friends with one or two employees?

2. What is the *rumor mill?* Why is it dangerous?

3. How does emotion affect the way we accept criticism?

4. What are some ways to keep your job interesting?

5. What are some positive ways of dealing with changes on the job?

Chapter Nine:

Self-Improvement— the Key to Success

Chapter Objectives

In this chapter you will:

1. Learn about the power of knowledge.

2. Review the effects of changes in the workplace and the need for constant improvement.

3. Learn about the importance of lifelong learning.

4. Learn the importance of self-improvement as a way of succeeding on the job.

5. Learn how to develop a plan for self-improvement.

6. Explore the many resources available to you for improving the skills you need on the job.

The student who stops learning when he or she leaves school will soon become uneducated.
                              Source unknown

The Age of Information has arrived. Today's employee must be willing to continue learning in order to stay competitive. Jobs are changing all the time. As new technology develops and new ways of doing business evolve, a successful worker must learn and grow in his or her work. Whether you are a salesperson in a retail store or an engineer in an aerospace, changes on the job are part of today's jobs. Those who don't learn and grow will be left behind.

Education doesn't end when you leave school.

Changes on the Job Require Workers to Continue Learning

Today's jobs are demanding. In the old assembly line way of doing things, a worker learned his or her job and then repeated it over and over. The job never changed. Sometimes a new idea would be introduced, but the change was usually a simple one. Generally, workers were only required to learn new information when they were promoted to a different job in the company—which didn't happen very often. In contrast, today's worker is expected to learn new jobs all the time.

Many employers want to **cross-train** their employees. Cross-training allows an employee to move from one area to another depending on the company's needs. For example, many banks teach their entry-level employees the skills needed to be tellers. Once they have learned to be tellers, they may be moved to the savings department where they help customers open new accounts or answer questions about their existing accounts. After that, they may be moved to the loan department to learn how to process new loans. Why would banks teach their employees so many different skills and move them around so much?

Bank managers know the company workload changes from time to time. During certain periods there may be more demand on the loan department than on the savings department. By training workers in both areas, managers can move employees around to meet the customers' needs. If a teller is sick and someone is needed at the teller window, an employee can be moved from the loan department to the teller window. If the bank is promoting new savings accounts and more workers are needed to help in that area, someone can be moved from another department to help customers open new savings accounts. These bank managers know that in order for companies to remain competitive, they must use efficient ways to provide goods and services. Cross-training workers is one way to improve efficiency.

Another way to remain competitive is to provide the best service possible. Today's companies are making major changes in the way they do business to make sure customers are getting good service. Employees receive extensive training in customer relations. Learning about company products, maintaining customer satisfaction, and learning how to talk to customers are only a few of the areas covered in customer training. Many employers expect the employee to know good customer relations before they start the job. It is up to the employee to learn these skills if he or she wants to succeed.

*Today's employees must learn
to do many jobs well.*

As our society becomes increasingly **global**, businesses will expect even more from their employees. The ways in which companies do business will change, the products will change, and the jobs will change. If you are going to succeed in this changing environment, you must find ways to educate yourself to meet the new requirements of your job. Many companies will provide some of the training you will need. If you are going to remain competitive as a worker, make sure to take advantage of the training that is available to you. Much of the training you will need may not be provided by your employer. You must find ways to obtain the training that is needed to upgrade your skills as your job changes. If you want to advance within your company or move to another job, you will need to learn the skills required for other jobs. This way you will be ready when the opportunity for advancement arises. Preparing yourself for your current job and for future jobs is a requirement these days.

Lifelong Learning

As you can see, educating yourself is a lifelong process. There are many reasons to continue learning, but the most important reason is to gain power. Not power to control people or take advantage of people, but the power people have when they know their job well and are respected by others. Tom Peters, a successful author who has written several books about successful companies says, "Knowledge is power." Think about that statement. If you are knowledgeable about your job, your company, and your fellow workers, you will be respected by those who work with you. If there is a problem, they will ask you for help. If they want to make a change, they will ask for your advice. That is a very powerful position in which to be. To gain that level of power and respect, you must earn it. You can earn it by educating yourself. What are some of the ways you can continue to learn and improve yourself?

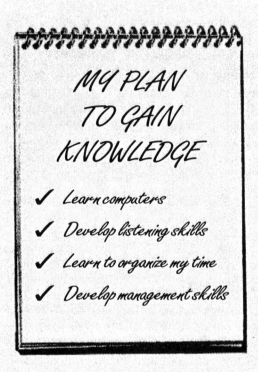

Develop a plan to become more knowledgeable.

Developing a Plan to Gain Knowledge

The first step in gaining knowledge is to determine what areas you want to study, and then develop a plan to reach a goal. In the next chapter, you will learn how to develop a plan for job success. As part of that plan, you may want to identify the type of training you will need and the best way to obtain that training. No matter what type of training you need, there are many ways to get it. The important thing is to take advantage of all the resources available to you. You may have to pay for some training, but much of what you need is available at little or no cost.

If you are reluctant to continue your education because you didn't enjoy school or didn't think it was important, you may find that learning about something that is important to you is different. When you realize the importance of improving your skills, learning becomes more interesting. The important thing is to get started.

Many workers don't realize all the resources available to them when it comes to learning new skills. No matter what kind of training you need, there is usually more than one source of training available to you. Let's look at some of the different ways you can acquire the knowledge you need.

How Community Classes Can Help

Most communities have night classes that anyone can attend. Community, state, and private colleges offer classes for a wide variety of subjects. Some public schools and parks departments offer community education classes too. To find out more about classes available in your community, watch your newspaper for class listings or notices of upcoming workshops. You also may want to contact the schools or agencies and get on their mailing lists so you can receive the latest information about their classes.

Sometimes community groups will offer workshops or classes on specific subjects which may interest you. Check your newspaper, or listen for information on the radio or television.

Learning From Magazines and Books

The number of magazines written for specific subject areas has increased dramatically in the past few years. Today, you can subscribe to magazines on everything from computers to self-improvement. Each month in the mail, you can receive up-to-date information on subjects that may help you on your job. Magazines allow you to learn about the latest events and developments that may affect you on the job in an age of rapidly changing information. In addition, magazines can provide you with information about other jobs you may want to investigate in the future.

Your local librarian may be able to help you find magazines that will be helpful to you. The library may even subscribe to one of these magazines. Some of the magazines that can be helpful to you are not found on the newsstands or in bookstores. You will need to subscribe to them or read them at the library. You will be amazed at the wide variety of subjects covered by magazines. Take the time to investigate this source of information.

Books are another excellent source of information. Because the workplace is changing so quickly, more and more books are being written on ways to be successful on the job. Again, a librarian can help you find the books that may be helpful to you. Visit your local bookstore and discover the many new books that have been published on self-improvement and human relations. Every book or magazine you read provides you with more information on how to keep up with the changes in your job.

Don't limit yourself in your search for information that will help you on the job. If you work for a retail store, find out what is happening in retail sales in general. You may discover trends in retail sales that can help you become a better employee. At some point you might have the opportunity to tell your boss about a trend that could help your company, or that would allow you to improve the way you do your job. Remember, you are seeking knowledge—knowledge that will help you do your current job better and that will prepare you for advancement. Learn everything you can about the business or industry in which your company competes.

Audio and Video Taped Instruction

Everyday, thousands of workers are learning new skills as they travel to and from work. One of the fastest growing techniques for learning is the use of audio cassette tapes. By listening to a learning tape while driving to work or school, today's workers and students are using time that is normally wasted to learn about a variety of subjects.

These learning tapes allow you to hear famous speakers discuss topics ranging from management techniques to ways of improving your memory. The majority of audio learning tapes cover subjects related to personal self-improvement—an important topic for any worker who wants to be successful on the job. Some of the helpful topics covered by audio training tapes include:

- Dealing with stress
- Accepting criticism
- Improving spelling
- How to assert yourself
- Psychology of achievement
- Time management
- Dealing successfully with difficult people
- The joy of working
- Improving your public speaking
- Management training
- Maintaining a positive attitude
- Foreign languages
- Interviewing for a job
- How to influence others

Of course, this is only a partial list of topics that can help you succeed in your job. Once you have identified subjects that will help you, find the audio tape that fits your needs. Then you can begin to learn important information during your free time. Think about how much time you spend in your car or doing jobs at home that could be used to learn new skills. Most self-improvement magazines will list sources of learning tapes. Many bookstores carry a good selection of audio learning tapes.

Video taped lessons are another relatively new source of information. Large quantities of training tapes currently are being produced by a number of companies, particularly in the areas of computer training and management. These tapes allow you to view lessons in your home. Then, you can go back and review the tape as many times as you wish. Video training tapes are available in most book stores, and some libraries have them available for checkout.

You can learn new skills in many different ways.

Gaining Experience Through Community Organizations

Community organizations offer excellent training opportunities for real-world skills. Every community or school has organizations that are involved in a variety of activities. By volunteering to work with one or more of these organizations, you can develop many skills that will help you become an effective employee. Furthermore, your work with these organizations demonstrates to employers that you are willing to work with others.

The opportunities for developing job skills range from managing budgets to public speaking. You can volunteer to help in areas that will benefit you the most. For example, if you need to become more comfortable working in groups, you might want to work with a committee to put on a benefit dinner for your organization. The committee will meet and develop plans for the benefit, dividing areas of responsibility among the members. As a member of that committee, you will learn valuable skills in group planning and division of responsibility.

Involvement in organizations and clubs also can offer valuable leadership experience. Many volunteers in community organizations and school clubs gain their first leadership experience as the chairpersons of committees. As time goes on, they gain confidence in their leadership skills, eventually becoming officers of the club or organization. Other learning opportunities available in clubs and organizations are budget development and record keeping. Many committees need to keep records of expenses and receipts. By involving yourself in these processes, you have the opportunity to learn how to develop budgets and keep financial records—a skill needed in many jobs. With time and experience, you may become the organization's treasurer. As treasurer, you will be involved with large budgets and substantial record-keeping activities.

*Joining clubs and organizations can help you
develop financial and record-keeping skills.*

Public speaking is another skill you can learn by helping in
your school or community. As a member of an active group,
you may be asked to give reports to the group about a planned
activity, or you may have the opportunity to talk to larger
groups about a project or effort on behalf of your organization.
These experiences will help develop communication skills you
can use on the job or as part of a future job assignment.

Community and club volunteer work has helped many workers advance quickly within an organization. Employers are
aware of the skills that can be learned as a part of a volunteer
organization. By volunteering for one of these groups you
accomplish two things: First, you are helping your school or
community; and second, you are developing valuable skills
that will help you now and in the future. Take advantage of

this source of skill development. Find out what clubs and organizations are available in your school and community. Once you have determined each group's type of activity, make a decision to get involved—you won't be sorry.

Learning From Others

One of the best ways to learn is to watch other people. If you have a chance to learn new skills from someone at work, take of advantage of this opportunity. Watch, participate, and learn from others. If you can come to work early or stay late to work with someone else, do it. Sometimes people pay a lot of money to learn information that may be available to you at work.

If you have friends who work at other jobs who could help you, learn as much as you can from them. The more you learn, the more knowledge you possess; the more knowledge you gain, the more valuable you are to your company. It is estimated that American companies spend thirty billion dollars a year in employee training. The more you can learn on your own, the further ahead you are on the job. If you are fortunate enough to work for a company that provides training, learn as much as you can on your own. Remember— *knowledge is power.* The more you learn about your job and your company, the more respect you will gain from your supervisor and those who work with you.

Study Questions

1. How have the jobs of today and tomorrow changed from the way they were performed in the past?

2. What is meant by *lifelong learning*? What does this mean to your future in the world of work?

3. What are some inexpensive ways you can learn new skills that will help you on the job?

4. Why is it important to develop a plan for acquiring new skills?

Chapter Ten:

Planning for Success

Chapter Objectives

In this chapter you will:

1. Learn the power of planning and positive thinking in achieving your goals.

2. Learn why it is important to be in control of your future on the job.

3. Discover why some employees move ahead on the job more quickly than others.

4. Learn how writing down your goals can help you succeed on the job.

5. Become aware of the importance of long-term planning.

*The message to us was universal; good jobs
will increasingly depend on people who can put
knowledge to work.*
                    The SCANS Report
                    A study of job skills for the future

Who is in Control?

Most adults spend at least thirty percent of their day at a job.
Do you think it is important to have a plan that will make
your work enjoyable and personally productive? You have two
choices regarding your job: You can put in your time and let
your job control you, or you can plan for success and take
control of your life while you are at work. Learn to develop a
plan for success on the job and take control of your life.

Most adults spend at least 30% of their life at work.

Your ability to succeed depends on your state of mind. Success does not just happen, it is the result of a person *believing* that he or she is going to be successful, and then working toward that success. Let's look at a recent example:

The words you are reading were first typed on the keyboard of a personal computer. That computer is a design developed by the IBM Corporation. A number of years ago there were only a few personal computers on the market. The most popular model was the Apple computer. IBM made large computers for big businesses, but did not have a small computer at a price small businesses or private individuals could afford. The market for small, low cost computers was growing. IBM needed to develop a small computer before the Apple computer became too popular. To stay competitive, IBM created a team to develop a small computer as quickly as possible.

The team began working on the development of what was to become the IBM Personal Computer. In record time, the IBM team designed a small computer with a variety of new features that became an instant success. That success was the direct result of goal setting. The team believed they would succeed in developing a revolutionary new computer because they *planned for success*.

Not to be outdone by IBM, Apple Computer, Inc. set a goal to develop a computer that would do things the new IBM PC couldn't do. The result was the development of the Apple Macintosh computer. As you can see, success comes to those who *plan* and *believe* they will succeed.

Success doesn't just happen, you have to *make* it happen. Most workers don't plan for job success, they just *hope* they will be successful. Unfortunately, hoping for success is a very slow process that usually ends in frustration. A written plan for success gives you a tremendous advantage on the job.

The Importance of Planning and Preparation

Many of today's workers realize the importance of preparing themselves for advancement on the job. For example, a few years ago, entry-level office workers knew they had to learn to type in order to move ahead in the company. Without this skill, they were unprepared to take on the duties of a secretary. Back then, this one skill could get entry-level office workers a better job.

Today it is not that easy. Today's jobs are more complex and require a thorough study to determine what skills are necessary to advance within a company.

*Today's jobs require more skills
than jobs did a few years ago.*

If you were to look around an office right now, you would see a lot of people using computers to fulfill their duties more efficiently. From this, it might appear that learning to type on a computer would provide a person with the skills necessary for many office jobs; however, this is not true. Computers can do so many tasks; word processing, databases, desktop publishing, spreadsheets, graphics, etc., that learning to type on a computer is only the first step in becoming computer literate. In addition to learning how to operate different types of computers, today's office workers also must learn how to use the computer programs that are used by the company.

An employee who takes only a quick look at the jobs in his or her company may not realize what is involved in getting ahead in today's workplace. After learning to type on a computer, a worker may find he or she learned this skill using a word processing program that is different from the one used at work. He or she would then be unprepared to compete for a job using computers within that company. People who have experience using a particular computer program will have an advantage over those who do not.

Steve started working for Allied Industries about four months before Ramona did. Steve is an **ambitious** person and wants to get ahead. When he first started with the company, he was taken on a tour of the facility. As he walked from department to department, he noticed that many computers were being used on the job. Steve had learned a little about computers in high school, but not enough to say he was good with computers. After several weeks on the job he realized that if he was going to get ahead at Allied Industries, he was going to have to learn more about computers.

While watching television, Steve saw an advertisement for computer classes at the local college. A computer class was just what Steve needed, so he signed up for a twelve week course in word processing. When he had completed the class, Steve felt he was ready for a job using computers.

Ramona also noticed all the computers in use at Allied Industries. She too, had learned a little about computers in high school. There was no question in Ramona's mind, but that she was going to have to learn more about computers. Within the first week at Allied Industries, Ramona was asking questions about the computers being used in her department. What would she have to learn in order to use those computers? She went to other departments and spoke with the computer operators. Soon she discovered that some departments used different computers than others. She also found that some computer operators were using different programs than others.

As she learned more about the company and its many job opportunities, Ramona focused upon the jobs for which she thought she was best qualified. Finally, she identified two jobs to which she would like to transfer when there was an opening. Each of those jobs required computer skills. Ramona found that she would have to learn how to use word processing and spreadsheet programs for one job, and a desktop publishing program for the other job.

After work, Ramona went to the local college and looked at the schedule of classes for the next term. She found that both word processing and desktop publishing classes were listed, so she signed up for both. The spreadsheet class was not offered until the next term. Ramona completed both classes. At work, she asked if she could use the computers after work to practice the skills she was learning in college. The next term Ramona completed the spreadsheet class. Whenever she got a chance, she would use the computers at work to keep improving the skills she had learned.

About once every week, Steve would check the bulletin board in the personnel office for job openings. One day, there was a listing that looked like just what he wanted. The pay was better and it would be a good advancement. The job was similar to his but required the use of a computer. He filled out the transfer form and waited to hear from the personnel office.

Ramona saw the same job listing and applied for a transfer too. She felt good about her **qualifications** because she had spoken to the people in that department and knew what was required to be successful on the job. Furthermore, she had learned that some jobs in that department were changing and would require more computer skills—skills she had learned.

As Steve waited in the personnel office for his job interview, he visited with the other candidates applying for the same job. They seemed like nice people. One candidate told Steve that he learned how to use computers in high school, but hadn't touched one in two years. Steve felt like that put him one up because he had taken a computer class last year.

Steve's interview surprised him. Besides the personnel manager, a department supervisor also was present. Both managers asked him questions about his experience with the company and the computer class he took in college. At the end of the interview, the personnel manager told Steve they would let him know about the job by the end of the week.

Ramona listened carefully as the personnel manager asked her questions about her computer experience. He seemed impressed that Ramona had developed computer skills on her own and used those skills as often as possible. The department manager asked her if she knew anything about database software. Ramona said she didn't, but was anxious to learn. The personnel manager told her they would let her know about the job by the end of the week.

On Friday, Steve was informed that he was being recommended for the transfer. Ramona heard from the personnel manager the same day.

> The personnel manager and department supervisor were so impressed with Ramona's personal effort, they offered her a different job than the one for which she had applied. A position was going to open in a month and they wanted Ramona to fill the position. The new job would be two steps above her current job and she would get a large increase in pay. In addition, Allied Industries would send Ramona to school to learn database software because it would be used in her new job.

Steve and Ramona each benefitted from preparing themselves for future jobs. However, in comparing Ramona's progress to that of Steve, there was a major difference.

To understand why Ramona benefitted the most, we need to look at the steps she took to prepare for the future:

1. Ramona didn't look at just one phase of the company's operation, she looked at jobs in other departments.

2. She asked questions to find out as much information as she could.

3. She looked at all the potential jobs and determined the ones for which she could best qualify.

4. She developed a plan to gain the skills she needed when one of those jobs became available.

5. She gained the skills she needed and remained flexible enough to learn a new skill when it was needed.

Steve improved his situation too, but not as dramatically as Ramona did. The problem with Steve's approach was that it stopped short of being a real plan for success. He did not set a specific goal, and failed to research the specific skills that would be required for the job. If he had taken the same steps Ramona did, he may have received the higher paying job because he had **seniority**. Furthermore, it was fortunate for Steve that another job became available; if it hadn't, Ramona would have been awarded the position that was given to Steve because she was more prepared.

Developing a Plan for Success

The first step in developing a plan for success on the job is to list what you would like to accomplish on the job. Here are some questions to help you develop that list:

1.   What do you want to learn about your company?

2.   What are some of the techniques you have learned (in this book and elsewhere) that you would like to use to succeed on the job?

3.   What opportunities for advancement are available to you?

4.   What skills do you need to develop for future job opportunities in your company?

5.   Do you want to move into management in the future?

As you develop your own list of job success activities, you will get more ideas for ways to work toward success on the job. Don't worry if your list of ideas seems long, as you develop your plan you will be able to shorten the list by combining your ideas. List ideas as they come to you. Don't worry about how difficult or easy they may be. The key to this process is getting your ideas down on paper.

Here is a list of ideas that someone might develop:

- Develop skills needed to advance on the job.
- Get to know my boss better.
- Identify a mentor.
- Identify an advocate.
- Learn more about the company.
- Visit other departments.
- Get to know other employees better.
- Take a public speaking class.
- Learn to do my job better.
- Take a supervision class.
- Develop a communication network.
- Develop ways to blow my own horn.
- Make a list of skills I need to advance on the job.
- Learn the formal and informal chain of command.
- Develop good listening skills.
- Avoid negative thinkers.
- Identify positive thinkers in the company.
- Visit all parts of the company.

Look at the list again. Can any of these ideas be grouped together? Let's see what we can combine...

Personal skill development
> Take a supervision class
> Develop good listening skills
> Develop skills needed to advance on the job
> Take a public speaking class
> Learn my job better
> Make a list of the skills I need to advance on the job

Working with others at work
> Identify a mentor
> Identify an advocate
> Get to know co-workers better
> Get to know my boss better
> Develop a communication network
> Learn the formal and informal chain of command
> Avoid negative thinkers
> Identify positive thinkers

Know the company
> Learn more about the company
> Visit other departments
> Visit all parts of the company

Recognition on the job
> Develop ways to blow my own horn

Do you see how various ideas can be grouped together? You might group them differently, or put the same idea in more than one group. Group your ideas in whatever way is best for you. Combining ideas will help you identify your job goals as well as the steps you need to take to reach those goals.

Now take one of those groups and use it to develop a goal for success on the job. For instance, using the group labeled *personal skill development*, you might create a goal to develop the skills you will need to help you qualify for advancement in the company.

In order to reach that goal, you need to develop short-term goals. Those short-term goals would be the skills you need to meet your long-term goal. Three of those goals are found in the list on the previous page; however, you may not have thought of all the skills you will need. List the skills you need to do your job better and to advance to other jobs. Here is an example of how the second list might look:

Skills needed to do a better job and to advance to other jobs

    Effective listening
    Public speaking
    Word processing (or other computer skills)
    The ability to manage others
    Better writing techniques
    The ability to ask questions when I don't
      understand directions
    The ability to keep a positive attitude
    Leadership techniques

Now you have a list of skills that can lead to the achievement of your long-term goal. You may find it difficult to work on all your short-term goals at once. If this happens, work on the most important ones first, and add others as you begin to reach your short-term goals.

This example is the first step in developing a plan for success on the job. As each long-term goal is set and the short-term goals are identified, they will be added to the plan.

Each person's plan will be different because the plan is designed to meet the specific needs of the individual. If we use the groups listed above, a plan for success on the job might look like this:

PLAN FOR SUCCESS ON THE JOB

		Goal Completed
Long-Term Goal:	Develop the skills I will need to help me qualify for advancement in the company.	
Short-Term Goals:	Learn and practice one good listening skill each week.	(x)
	Take a public speaking class.	( )
	Take a class on technical writing.	(x)
	Take a leadership role at work at least once a week.	( )
Long-Term Goal:	Develop a support network at work.	
Short-Term Goals:	Identify a mentor.	( )
	Identify an advocate.	(x)
	Develop a communication network.	( )
	Determine my boss' management style.	(x)
	Help my boss at least once a month.	( )
Long-Term Goal:	Be sure I receive recognition for my efforts at work.	
Short-Term Goal:	Share my job related efforts with a co-worker or manager at least once a month.	( )

The second part of the plan for success on the job is to
identify the steps necessary to reach the short-term goals.
In Chapter Seven, you learned that reaching a goal requires
more than just stating what you hope to accomplish. To be
successful, you must develop a plan to reach that goal. The
plan you develop will enable you to overcome obstacles you
may encounter as you work toward reaching your goal. If you
develop a goal to develop a support network at work, it might
look like this:

Long-Term Goal: Develop a support network at work.

Short-Term Goal: Identify a mentor (s).

Obstacles to overcome: I am not good at meeting new people.

Overcoming Obstacles: I will ask how long they have worked at the company or what they do on their job. I may open the conversation with subjects that may be of common interest to both of us.

Measure progress: Meet at least one new employee each week and maintain contact with them.
Develop a list of employees who have skills I wish to learn.

Personal Rewards: I will identify a mentor (s) and learn a great deal about my job in a short period of time.

Positive Affirmations: Meeting others will be fun & rewarding.
Others will like me because I show an interest in them.
I will become a better employee.

Visualization:

Your own plans may not involve as many steps as this example. Some of your short-term goals may be simple and easy to accomplish. The important thing is to think about what you want to accomplish and *write it down*. As your situation changes, adjust your plan. Accomplish your goals and set new ones.

Successful goal setters set new goals and stretch their limits. Everyone is capable of doing more than they think they can. The best way to reach your potential is to challenge yourself continually. *CHALLENGE YOURSELF* and learn to develop a plan for success on the job.

Long-Term Plans

Does all this planning seem like a lot of work? It is! Successful people know they must work hard to succeed. If you are going to be successful on the job, you need to put in time and effort to assure your success. Most people spend years in school preparing themselves for success in life and on the job.

After years of education, doesn't it make sense to develop a plan to use the skills you have learned? Doesn't it make sense to determine the additional skills you will need to succeed on the job, and then learn them as quickly and efficiently as possible? The answer to all these questions is "Yes," unless you don't care about your future. Do some extra work now to make life on the job a lot easier in the future.

Study Questions

1. How can you control your job and not let it control you?

2. What is a plan for success on the job? How can you develop one?

3. How do long-term goals and short-term goals differ?

4. Why will working hard on a plan now pay off for you in the future?

Chapter Eleven:

Becoming a Supervisor

Chapter Objectives

In this chapter you will:

1. Explore the possibility of moving into a management position.

2. Review the questions to consider when making the decision to move into management.

3. Find out where to find the training you need to become a good manager.

4. Learn how to let the company know you want to become a manager.

I will study and get ready, and some day my chance will come.
                                    Abraham Lincoln

Where to Go Next?

When you are hired to work for a company, you start out at a beginning wage. As you gain experience, your wages increase until you reach the highest wage level for your job. When you reach the top of your wage level, there are usually two ways to increase your wages. In some cases, you may be able to transfer to another job in the company that pays a higher wage. The other choice may be to move into management.

Managers usually make more money than hourly employees. Some hourly employees decide to move into management to take on new challenges as supervisors. Others become managers to become part of the company's decision-making process. Whatever your reason for considering a move to management, a decision should be made only after careful **consideration** of all the facts related to such a promotion.

Preparing for the opportunity to move into management is one more step toward controlling your life at work. In this chapter you will learn ways to decide if management is right for you. You also will find out what you need to do to be ready to take on the responsibilities of a manager if such an opportunity comes your way.

Supervising employees requires special skills. If you want to become a manager and you do not have these skills, you must find some way to acquire them. Asking yourself some questions can help you **assess** your ability to manage others.

Asking the Right Questions

Are people important to me? As an employee, you probably work with the same group of people every day, and you have a common interest in your work or projects. As a supervisor, you will work with people in different levels of authority in a variety of situations: In the morning you may help a new employee learn about his or her job; two hours later you may be talking to an employee about his or her poor performance that month; and before noon, you may meet with other supervisors to make decisions affecting your department and others. All this interaction takes place in the first four hours of the day! If you like people and want to see them become successful, this will be a challenge for you. If you only like working with people who appear to like you, supervision may be very uncomfortable for you.

A supervisor needs to deal with many different situations.

Am I a leader? Being a supervisor is very different from being an hourly employee. As an hourly employee, you may have the opportunity to take a leadership role for a while, but at other times you must follow the directions of your boss. Supervisors take leadership roles every day. They have the responsibility to complete an assignment and they must get it done with the help of their employees. If they are good leaders, the work will be done correctly and on time. If not, they have not done their jobs. If you want to be a successful supervisor, you must be a good leader.

Do I like planning and organizing? A supervisor's job involves a great deal of planning. Good supervisors know how to plan the work that needs to be done and assign the right person to each job. As assignments change, supervisors must adjust work schedules and employee assignments. Unlike an employee who is given assignments by someone else, the supervisor must make it all happen on time all the time without direct help from his or her own supervisor. If you like to organize and plan, you have an important skill that is necessary in order to be a good supervisor.

Am I afraid of paperwork? Supervisors must complete a lot of paperwork. Workers must be evaluated and recommended for advancement, vacations must be planned, overtime pay must be calculated, and company production records must be maintained to evaluate progress. Additionally, production schedules must be set, supplies must be tracked, and reports required by state and federal agencies must be completed. The clerical staff does much of this, but the supervisor must **initiate** the process and make sure the documents are accurate.

Supervisors have to do a lot of paperwork.

Can I accept responsibility? Supervisors are responsible for the operation of a department or section of a company. Each day the workers in that department or section work on assignments that have been planned by the supervisor. If the plan is good, the work gets done. If the plan is not good or an employee does not carry his or her share of the load, the work may not get done. When the work does not get done, the supervisor can't blame the employees. He or she must accept the responsibility for lack of performance and make the necessary changes to correct the problem.

Like everyone, supervisors sometimes make mistakes. After all, they must make a variety of decisions every day; therefore, it is not surprising that occasionally the wrong decision is made. A good supervisor is not afraid to admit he or she has made a mistake. Can you accept the responsibility if you make a mistake or things don't go as planned?

Can I let others do it? One of the problems new supervisors **encounter** is how to **delegate** responsibility. As a worker, you have control of the work assigned to you. A supervisor must make sure the work gets done, but he or she can't do it alone. Supervisors must trust that others will do it the way they want it done. This can be difficult for someone who takes pride in his or her work. Can you trust someone else to do it right?

Developing the Skills of a Supervisor

If you have not been a supervisor before, it may difficult to answer some of these questions. Many new supervisors never have a chance to find out if they have the right skills to be supervisor until after they are promoted. Unfortunately, it is not uncommon for a new supervisor to discover he or she is not ready for the job until it is too late. This can be a very difficult situation. He or she either must learn how to be a supervisor, or go back to being an hourly employee. Sometimes, a new supervisor will leave the company simply because he or she is too embarrassed to admit that the job was too difficult. Obviously, it is better to be prepared for a supervisor's job before it is offered to you. If you would like to become a supervisor, develop a plan to help you reach that goal.

If offered a job, will you be ready to make the right decision?

Learning to Be a Supervisor

There is nothing wrong with not wanting to become a supervisor. Many employees are challenged and happy with their jobs. However, if an employee does not at least *think* about becoming a supervisor, he or she may miss an opportunity for personal growth as well as a better income. How can you find out if you would like to be a supervisor?

To become a good supervisor, you will need to learn the proper skills. Reading a book or taking a class on supervision are both good ways to learn the skills you will need. There are many good books and magazines on supervision. Your librarian can help you find written materials to study. As you learn about the skills, ask yourself if you possess them. If not, you may want to set a goal to develop the skills you need. Remember, reading and learning about supervision is only the first step in developing the necessary skills. Now you must find a way to put the newly learned supervision techniques to work.

Learning From Organizations

As you learned in Chapter Nine, one of the best ways to learn people skills is to get involved with organizations or clubs in your school or community. Clubs and organizations usually have several projects on which members work. Working on a club project is a great way to practice the skills you want to improve. The larger the club or organization, the larger the projects. If you need to develop a number of skills, start with a small project and concentrate on one or two skills at a time. Take on more difficult assignments as you gain confidence in your leadership skills.

Working with clubs and organizations provides you with opportunities to become a leader, make mistakes, and learn in a situation that are non-threatening. If you make a mistake while you are learning within an organization, others will be likely to understand. However, if you try to develop your leadership skills at work and make a mistake, it might affect your job. By working with a volunteer group, you can learn from others and develop the skills you need. Many successful people volunteer their time for community organizations and clubs. By working with these successful people, you can develop mentors away from work.

As you gain confidence in yourself, expand your involvement in the organization. The treasurer of an organization gains experience in handling money and working with budgets. Project chairpersons organize projects to reach group goals. They learn how to motivate volunteers to achieve the goals of a project. Secretaries take the notes for the organization and are responsible for keeping records. As you can see, an organization's officers make decisions that affect the entire organization. This is valuable experience!

If you take time to develop a plan for moving up to supervision, you could include various positions of responsibility in a club or organization. Start with the office of treasurer or secretary. Then, as you gain experience, you may consider moving up to vice-president or president. It looks very good on your resume if you have demonstrated leadership skills in a club or community organization. Employers know that a person who can motivate volunteers in a community organization is likely to be able to motivate paid employees.

Involvement with organizations away from work is just as important as reading books about supervision. The organization you join will help you practice the skills you read about in books or learn about in classes. As in everything you do, plan your involvement in an organization. Investigate the clubs and groups that are available to you. What are they doing? Are they involved in important projects? All organizations are looking for new members. Don't jump at the first group that invites you to join—attend a meeting and ask questions. Visit more than one group. If you are going to donate your time, you may as well benefit as much as possible for your volunteer efforts. Pick a group that provides opportunities for you to learn the skills you need, and that serves a cause that interests you. Once you have picked an organization, make a commitment to do your best. Remember, you only get as much out of something as you are willing to commit.

Does your new club have any important activities?

Learning at Work

You can learn about supervision at work by watching others. Watch your own supervisor and other supervisors in your company. Develop good **observation** skills by studying the way supervisors deal with different situations. Ask yourself questions about the way certain decisions were made. Get to know your boss, and volunteer for assignments that involve responsibility. If you do something wrong, ask your boss how he or she would have handled the situation.

As you learn techniques at work, try them in your club or organization. Take every opportunity to learn new skills and practice whenever you get the chance. The old saying, "Practice makes perfect," is true. As you gain confidence, look for ways to prove your leadership skills. If the organization needs someone to chair a committee, accept the challenge. If the boss wants an employee to work with someone else, volunteer. Every new experience will expand your people skills. Listen and ask questions—that's the fastest way to learn about your job and other people's jobs. Just be careful not to ask too many questions at once; some people get impatient if they are asked too many questions. Learn as much as you can about supervision and practice what you learn. If you do this, you will be prepared when the opportunity to become a supervisor is presented to you.

Letting Your Company Know About Your Plans

"I don't understand it, they promoted Leslie to department supervisor! Didn't they know I wanted to be supervisor?" It is not unusual to hear this kind of statement in the workplace. Many workers assume the decision makers in the company know what kind of promotion each employee wants. This is a mistake. Employers must be told when an employee is interested in a promotion to management. How can you let your boss know you want to be a supervisor?

In Chapter Four you learned to blow your own horn. Letting your boss know you are interested in a management position is part of this process. If you have developed a communication network, let others know you are taking college classes in management, or that you are president of a local community organization. Without sounding like you are bragging, you can let the appropriate people know your election as president is part of your plan to prepare yourself for a management position. If it is appropriate, ask your boss's opinion on something you have read or learned about management.

Let people know you are developing
leadership skills — blow your own horn!

It is important to know the people you speak to at work. This makes it possible for you to pick the right time and place to bring up ideas or ask questions. For example, if you saw a television program about changes in management styles, how could you use that information to let your boss know about your interest in supervision?

One of the best ways to give people information is to ask for their help. If a person thinks you are asking them for advice, they will be more **receptive** to your information than if you try to tell them something. Look at the following example.

> Bruce knows that his boss, Virginia, doesn't like people telling her what they want. Virginia is a nice person, she just isn't open to people saying they want something. Because Bruce knows this about Virginia, he must think of a different approach to let her know about his interest in becoming a supervisor.
>
> At lunch, Bruce mentioned to Virginia that he had seen a program on public television about changes in management styles. He went on to say he was just elected president of a local organization, and was thinking about using some of the techniques he saw on television to manage the club. Then he asked his boss her opinion about his plan.

It doesn't really matter if Virginia agreed or disagreed with the ideas or techniques Bruce mentioned. The most important thing is that Bruce let his boss know about his interest in becoming a supervisor. He gave his boss information without telling her directly that he would like to be a supervisor. If Bruce had a different boss, he may have been able to tell him or her directly that he was interested in becoming a supervisor.

As time goes on, Bruce will use other situations to let Virginia know he is learning about supervision in college. If she never had formal training in supervision, he may not bring up his management class, but instead, emphasize his management experience as president of a community organization. The important thing to remember is to pass on information in an appropriate manner.

When a management position becomes available, it is important that the people who make the decisions in the company know of your plan to become a supervisor. If they know you are working toward that goal, you may get the job. If they don't know about you or your plans, someone else probably will get it.

If you are offered a job as a supervisor, will you be ready to make the right decision?

Study Questions

1. What questions do you need to ask yourself if you are thinking of becoming a manager?

2. How can volunteering to help a community organization help you develop the skills you need to become a good manager?

3. How can you let the decision makers in your company know you want to become a manager?

4. What is wrong with just reading a book about management to learn good management skills?

Chapter Twelve:

Should You Change Jobs?

Chapter Objectives

In this chapter you will:

1. Explore the reasons for changing employers.

2. Ask yourself questions to determine if you have tried to overcome work problems.

3. Discover the importance of leaving your company on good terms.

4. Learn to develop a plan for finding employment with another company.

5. Find ways to make the move to another job a positive experience.

*The average worker will change jobs seven times
in their working lifetime.*

Bill Clinton,
President of the United States

It's Practically Inevitable

At some time in your career you will probably leave one company and go to work for another. The reasons for leaving a
company vary from situation to situation, but problems with
management, fellow workers, or company rules may create
difficult situations that cannot be resolved in any other way.

Situations Beyond Your Control

Companies change over the years. New management may be
hired, and you may be assigned a new boss. Sometimes, the
wrong people are promoted—people who don't have the right
skills for the job. If the company doesn't see the problem or is
unwilling to change the situation, you may want to look for
another job.

Similarly, you may find that you just can't work with another
employee. This doesn't necessarily mean that you have to
change jobs. However, if you make every effort to solve your
differences with that person and the problems still exist, and
you have investigated all your options (including changing
jobs within the company), it may be best to find another job
in a different company.

The chances of reaching your career goals may be limited by the size of the company for which you work. Working for a small company can be a wonderful experience. You have the opportunity to work with and get to know everyone in the company. However, small companies sometimes have limited opportunities for advancement. As you learn your job and look for other opportunities within the company, you may find that there are none.

Sometimes seniority rules, company policy, and labor contracts may require another person for a job, even if you have worked hard to prepare for the job yourself. If this happens, your career goals with that company may be limited.

Economic factors can also force companies to cut back on promotions. If the company can't overcome the economic problems, some employees may even lose their jobs.

American
Industries
to Lay Off 700
Employees!

Leaving a job may be beyond your control.

No matter what your reasons are for considering a job change, the way in which you leave a company can have a major impact on your success in finding another job. Successful job changes require planning. This chapter will explore some of the ways you can plan for a successful future.

Have You Tried Everything?

Quitting your job is a serious decision. Sometimes employees become upset with their bosses and quit their jobs in anger. When someone quits a job in frustration or anger, the decision is based on emotion rather than common sense. This is a major error that can create a problem for the future.

Your former bosses are your references for future jobs. If you leave your job in anger, your former boss may not give you the best recommendation. On the other hand, if you were a good employee and left your job on good terms, your former boss will give you a good **recommendation**. Remember—the quality of your recommendations can make the difference between being turned down for a position and being hired. Before you leave your job, you should make sure your decision is a responsible one. Ask yourself the following questions:

- Have I tried my best to solve the problems?
- If I wait to tell my boss I am leaving, will I change my mind?
- Have I thought about alternatives to leaving my job?
- Do I have a plan for finding another job?
- Am I prepared to move to another job?

Ask yourself these questions to be sure you have done everything possible to make the right decision. Solving a problem between you and your boss is a lot easier than finding another job and starting over. If you cannot get along with another worker, have you looked into transferring to somewhere else in the company? The other person may not realize you are uncomfortable in your relationship with him or her. Talking to that person about the problem is a lot easier than finding another job.

Waiting a week to tell your boss you are quitting can help if you are upset. This keeps your emotions from speaking for you. If you wait a week, your attitude may change and the crisis may no longer exist. However, if after waiting a week, you still feel you must leave, you should prepare yourself for quitting your job.

The Danger of Burning Your Bridges

When an army is leaving an area, they burn the bridges behind them so the enemy can't follow them across rivers. The only problem is, the army can't turn around and go back because the bridges are gone. Employees sometimes make the mistake of burning their bridges behind them. Quitting a job in anger makes it difficult to go back and ask your boss for a good recommendation.

Don't burn your bridges behind you!

Part of planning to leave a company is making sure you can go back and ask for help. No matter why you quit a job, it is important to leave on good terms. That means letting your boss know in advance that you are leaving, and indicating a willingness to help the company fill your position. Give your boss a two to four week notice. This will give your boss enough time to find and train a replacement. You may be asked to train your replacement. If so, help as much as possible. Your cooperation may benefit you in the future.

Always give **adequate** notice and be as helpful as possible when you tell your boss you are leaving—even if you already have another job. In another two years you may be looking for yet another job and need a good recommendation. If you treat people fairly, they will usually treat you the same.

Planning for the Future

It would be nice if we could stay at our jobs forever. We would always know what is expected of us, and we would always know our co-workers. But situations change, and we must learn to change with them. It is estimated that the average worker will change jobs seven times during his or her working life. Does that surprise you? These changes are not always the result of problems with bosses or co-workers; often, they are due to changes within the company. Therefore, even if you get along fine with your boss and the people you work with, statistics show that you are likely to change jobs at some point in your career. To prepare for the future, you should plan for those changes.

Anytime you change jobs, whether you are moving from one part of a company to another or leaving the company completely, you will be asked questions about your previous work. One way to develop a plan for changing jobs is to develop the answers to those questions long before you change jobs. Let's look at some typical interview questions asked of people applying for a new job.

- Tell me about your work experience.

- What did you accomplish in your last job?

- How did you get along with your former boss and co-workers?

- Tell me about your studies in school.

- What special training have you had for this job?

- What did you like most about your last job?

- What was your single most important accomplishment on your last job?

- What was the toughest problem you had to solve?

- What were your major responsibilities in your last position?

As you look at this list, imagine yourself answering these questions three or four years after working for the same company. Something you did several years earlier might be a good answer to one of these questions.

Will you be prepared for your next job interview?

You might accept an assignment in your first year of work that demonstrates your ability to assume responsibility. Although this would probably be a **milestone** for you at the time, you may not remember that assignment three years later in an interview. However, if you develop a list of your accomplishments at work, you will be able to review that list before your interviews. What about the question regarding your accomplishments on the job? Wouldn't it be difficult to answer that question if you didn't review a list of your accomplishments first? You bet it would!

When you are called for an interview, you don't know what questions you will be asked. To be successful in your interview, you will need to review your past job history as well as any training you may have received. Keep a record of any workshops or seminars you attend. Maintaining a list of your accomplishments at work will help prepare you for the future.

Working well with co-workers is a skill employers like to see. When you work on projects that demonstrate your ability to work with others, add them to your list. You will be able to share that information with your interviewer in the future. Interviews can be stressful; it is easy to forget important events of the past. Preparing yourself for future job changes will make your transition easier and more productive.

Changing Jobs

Usually you will have some control over the situation when you leave a job. The amount of time you have to find another job will depend on your reason for departure. For instance, if you want to **relocate**, you probably have as much time as you need; you simply wait to move until you have found a new job. However, there are times when you have no choice about your job change; you may lose your job due to **reorganization**, budget cuts, or changes in company ownership. Even if you have been a good employee, you may be caught in one of these changes. These are situations that are out of your control. If this happens, you may feel angry and frustrated over losing your job; but remember, regardless of your reason for leaving, it is important to leave in a positive manner and be prepared for finding future work.

Once you realize that a job change is **imminent**, the first thing you will need to do is find another job. There are a number of books on the market that can help you prepare resumes, identify potential jobs, and learn how to interview. State and private employment agencies can help you locate potential jobs, but before you start a full scale job search you should do some things at work that can help you in your search.

Your information network and contacts at work may be able to help you find another job. If you are looking for a job similar to the one you currently hold, people you work with may know of opportunities elsewhere. Salespeople, **vendors**, inspectors, and others who visit your company may know of job opportunities in other companies they visit. Take a few minutes to make a list of people you contact who may be able to help you. Unless your plans to change jobs cannot be discussed with others, let others know what you would like to do.

Let others know you are looking for another job.

Co-workers have family members and friends who work for other companies. If your co-workers know what you can do and what you would like to do, they may be able to provide you with valuable information regarding opportunities in other companies. After all, if you have helped them in the past, they are likely to help you. Making a job change requires the same kind of preparation as developing career plans.

Change is not easy. The best way to deal with change is to prepare for it. When you reach the point where you need to make a change, having a plan will make the decision easier. Knowing you are in control of your job and your future allows you to make better choices and gives you self-confidence. Having confidence in yourself at work affects all aspects of your life. Plan for success on the job and discover your own personal success.

Study Questions

1.   What situations might cause you to change employers?

2.   What is wrong with telling your boss what you don't like about the company and quitting with no notice?

3.   Why is it important to include job changes in your long-term planning for job success?

4.   What are some ways to find another job if you decide to change employers?

Glossary

Accommodating: willing to help. Making an extra effort to adjust and work with others.

Accomplish: to succeed in doing something; to finish a task.

Achievement: something that is accomplished or finished through effort.

Adequate: enough for a particular requirement; reasonably sufficient (i.e., telling a person about your plans far enough in advance to let them plan accordingly).

Advocate: a person who speaks in a positive way about another person; someone who works for another's success. On the job, this may be another employee, a supervisor, or other interested person.

Affirmations: positive assertions; statements that confirm your ability to accomplish a goal and obtain the rewards associated with that goal.

Affirmative action: an active effort to improve the hiring, employment, and educational opportunities for minority groups and women.

Ambitious: possessing the desire to succeed. On the job this could mean striving to learn, grow, and do the best you can.

American system of manufacture: a system for producing manufactured products in which workers made various parts of a product separately. Each worker made a large number of the same part. Someone else would then be responsible for assembling some or all of the parts. This system allowed companies to manufacture products rapidly.

Anticipate: to plan ahead; to foresee and/or deal with in advance.

Appreciate: to recognize and value a person's efforts.

Apprentice: a worker who learns his or her skills through practical experience while working under the direction of a more experienced worker. Long ago, workers had to work under this system for a specific length of time before they were allowed to work on their own. In many cases, a worker would be an apprentice for several years before they were considered ready to complete all tasks by themselves.

Assembly line: a manufacturing system in which a product is built in stages as it moves from one worker to the next in a direct line. Each worker adds a part to the product until it is completed.

Assess: to determine the importance, size, or value of something (i.e., assessing one's skills with respect to a certain task.)

Attitude: a state of mind or feeling regarding some matter, that may influence your actions (i.e., the way you think about your job affects the way you do it).

Attributes: the personal strengths of an individual; an inherent characteristic.

Auditor: an accountant or bookkeeper who examines a company's financial records for accuracy.

Authoritarian style of management: a style of management in which a manager expects workers to follow directions and not ask questions. Workers are not encouraged to make suggestions or find better ways of doing their job.

Authoritarian: one who favors blind submission to authority.

Authority: the power to influence or command thought, opinion, or behavior.

Automate: to convert to largely automatic operation. Automating a business would involve shifting from the use of workers to a process that uses automatic machines and workers or just automatic machines to produce products or services.

C

Chain of command: a process by which information or directions are passed from one level to the next in an organization. Typically, information moves from the top level of management down various levels of management to the first line workers at the bottom of the organization.

Commercial: a term that applies to products made for sale to individuals or companies.

Commitment: a pledge to do something. This may involve applying all your abilities to reach a goal.

Compatibility: the ability to work and get along with others.

Compromise: a settlement in differences in which both sides make concessions.

Consideration: a matter thought about and weighed when formulating an opinion or a plan.

Consumer: a person who purchases products or services for his or her own use.

Cooperation: the action of working with others to reach a common goal.

Criteria: the requirements for making a decision.

Cross-train: a process in which companies train employees for various jobs within the organization. Workers who know different jobs can be moved on a temporary basis to areas in the company where more help is needed.

Cultivate: to promote growth and development.

D

Deadline: a point in time at which a task must be completed.

Deductible: that portion of the repair costs an owner must pay when an insured automobile is damaged; that portion of the costs of replacing stolen insured items an owner must pay. The insurance company pays the balance of costs after the owner's portion.

Delegate: to pass authority on to another (i.e., a manager may allow an employee to complete an assignment or task that is the direct responsibility of the manager).

Demonstrate: to show clearly; to prove through reason or evidence.

Distraction: a situation or problem that keeps you from concentrating on your work.

E

Eavesdropper: one who listens secretly to something that is said in private.

Economic: of, relating to, or based upon the production, distribution, and consumption of products or services.

Efficiency: effective operation as measured by a comparison of product and cost (as in energy, time and money); the quality that describes the completion of a task in a way that requires the least amount of time with the least number of steps.

Encounter: to come upon unexpectedly (i.e., a person, problem, or situation).

Entrepreneur: a person who organizes, operates, and assumes the risks for a business venture.

Export: transporting products out of a country for sale or trade in other countries.

F

Feedback: receiving information from a person regarding an idea, proposal, or suggestion you have made to him or her.

Fiber optic communications: a method of transferring large amounts of information using light transmitted through transparent cables at very high speeds. Replaced wire cable which carries less data at slower speeds.

G

Gender: relates to male or female.

Global: of or relating to the entire world.

Goal: the purpose for which an effort is directed. Unless some personal reward is involved, the effort may be limited.

I

Imminent: about to occur; impending.

Imported: bringing products into a country for sale or trade to residents of that country.

Indecision: the inability to make a decision regarding two or more courses of action.

Infer: to suggest, hint, or imply; the communication of information without making a direct statement.

Informal chain of command: a system of communication in a company or organization that differs from the established protocol of passing information from one level to the next lower level. It often emerges when a weak link appears in the normal flow of communication. The informal chain of command should not be confused with passing gossip from one person to another.

Initiate: to start a process or action; to take the lead in accomplishing a task.

Initiative: the power, ability, or instinct to begin or complete a task without being told what to do.

Insight: the ability to determine the true nature of a situation that may not be obvious to others.

Interest: money a bank pays customers for the use of their money; money a customer pays a bank for loaning them money. The amount of interest is based on a percentage of the total dollars borrowed or loaned.

Interfere: to get in the way of something; to hinder.

Internal conflict: conflict that exists inside you; a mental struggle resulting from incompatible or opposing needs, drives, wishes, or external and internal demands.

Interpersonal skills: the skills needed to work well with others; people skills.

J

Jeopardize: to expose to harm; to imperil.

M

Mediocrity: of moderate or low quality (i.e., not working at your best level).

Mentor: a teacher. A worker who shares his or her knowledge and experience in an effort to help another employee learn more quickly.

Merchant: a person whose job is to purchase products from a supplier or manufacturer and then sell them at a higher price to make a profit.

Milestone: a significant event in development (i.e., an important event in one's history or career).

Motivate: to create a desire to accomplish a goal or task.

O

Observation: a process in which a person watches, listens, and learns from others.

Obstacle: a barrier to achieving a goal.

Occupational revolution: Major changes in the workplace caused by technological and economic trends.

Optimist: a person who usually expects a favorable outcome.

Overreact: an inappropriately vigorous response to a situation.

P

Paraphrase: to repeat something someone has said in your own words; a way of being sure you understand what someone has said.

Participate: to take part; to join or share with others.

Participatory management: a style of management in which employees join with managers in making decisions.

Peer-praising: telling your boss or others about the good work one or more of your fellow workers has done.

Peer: a person with whom you work.

Pessimist: a person who consistently takes the negative view of a situation.

Potential: the ability or capacity for growth; a person's ability to accomplish a task.

Profitable: a situation in which the cost of operation is less than the money received for products or services provided.

Q

Qualifications: skills required for a specific job.

Qualified worker: a worker who has the skills and qualifications an employer needs.

Quality circles: a management system that allows a group of workers and supervisors to work in teams. Meeting on a regular basis, the teams work on solving production, service, or quality problems.

R

Rational: having logic and reason (i.e., dealing with a situation in a reasonable manner.)

Receptive: willing to accept ideas and suggestions.

Recession: a moderate temporary decline in economic activity; a condition that can cause employers to lay off workers.

Recommendation: a written or verbal statement of one's quality as a worker. Most companies will not hire a new employee without a good recommendation from a previous employer.

Refute: to show to be false or erroneous; to correct misinformation.

Reliability: the quality that allows a person to produce the same level of results again and again; dependability.

Relocate: to move to a new location.

Reorganization: a change in the way a company does business, or is structured. Many companies are eliminating various levels of management and workers. Changes usually are made to make a company more efficient and profitable.

Reputation: an opinion others may have about you that is based on your attitude and the quality of your work.

Responsive: readily reacting in an appropriate manner to suggestions, influences, appeals, or efforts.

Rumor mill: a gossip network in which information about the company or other employees is passed without regard to its accuracy.

S

Satellite communications: sending information from one point on the earth to another by a satellite in space. A signal is sent from one location to a satellite, and then from the satellite to another location.

Self-confidence: believing in one's ability to accomplish what they set out to complete.

Self-esteem: an attitude one has about oneself.

Seniority: refers to the length of time a person has been employed by a particular company. Seniority is often considered when evaluating a person for job advancement, promotions, pay raises and etc.

Sensitive: aware of how others may feel about themselves, others, or their job; tactful.

Sincerity: honesty regarding your actions and words; saying or doing things because they are the right thing to do, not because you want to impress others.

Standardized parts: a process in which one worker makes the same parts over and over in the same way.

Subtle: not immediately obvious; so slight as to be difficult to detect.

Systematic: an organized way of dealing with issues; a step by step process to address a situation or challenge.

T

Teamwork: work that is done by several employees joining forces to accomplish a task; work that involves cooperating with others in a give and take process that ends in the completion of a project or assignment.

Turnaround: in business, changing an unprofitable situation to one in which substantial profits are being made.

V

Vendors: individuals or companies that provide goods or services to companies.

Volunteer: offering to participate in an activity without being asked; offering to participate in an activity (usually that helps someone) without being paid.

Note: Adapted from *Webster's Ninth New Collegiate Dictionary*, Merriam-Webster, Inc., Springfield, MA, 1989.

Chapter Quotations

Chapter One
"Employee Involvement: The Quality Circle Process." *Vital Speeches of the Day*, (New York: The City News Publishing Co., July 1, 1988), vol. 54, 564.

Chapter Two
Thomas Jefferson, Third President of the United States, *The Edge: The Guide to Fulfilling Dreams, Maximizing Success and Enjoying a Lifetime of Achievement*, (Cleveland, OH: Getting the Edge Company, 1990), 4-12

Chapter Three
"Where Employees are Management," *BusinessWeek*, Special Edition on Reinventing America, 1992, 66.

Chapter Four
The Edge: The Guide to Fulfilling Dreams, Maximizing Success and Enjoying a Lifetime of Achievement, (Cleveland, OH: Getting the Edge Company, 1990), 1-4

Chapter Five
The Edge: The Guide to Fulfilling Dreams, Maximizing Success and Enjoying a Lifetime of Achievement, (Cleveland, OH: Getting the Edge Company), 1990, 2-4.

Chapter Six
Simpson's Contemporary Quotations, compiled by James B. Simpson, (Boston: Houghton Mifflin Co., 1988), 95.

Chapter Seven
Building a Quality Work Force, (Office of Public Affairs, Employment and Training Administration, U.S. Departments of Labor, Commerce, and Education, 1988), 16.

Chapter Eight
Building a Quality Work Force, (Office of Public Affairs,
Employment and Training Administration, U.S. Departments
of Labor, Commerce, and Education, 1988), 16.

Chapter Nine
Source unknown

Chapter Ten
"The SCANS Report," *A Scans Report for America 2000*,
(Secretary's Commission on Achieving Necessary Skills,
U.S. Department of Labor, June 1991), XV.

Chapter Eleven
H. P. Richter and W. C. Schwan, *Wiring Simplified*, (St. Paul,
MN: Park Publishing, Co., 1986), inside front cover.

Chapter Twelve
Speech by President Bill Clinton to a joint session of Congress.
February 17, 1993.

Index